DESIGN INTENT

in Creo Parametric

2nd Edition

By David Randolph Martin II

Chapters

Table of Contents

Table of Figures

Preface

> "You must know why things work on a starship."
>
> Captain James T. Kirk, Star Trek II: The Wrath of Khan

The Purpose of This Book

Design Intent forms the basis of the philosophy and operation of Creo Parametric, but most people don't understand what it is, how to build it into CAD models, and how to achieve the maximum benefit from using it in the product development process.

Creo Parametric provides organizations with the ability to design, analyze, and manufacture complex parts, assemblies, and products within a single modeling environment. Coupled with Windchill as a Product Lifecycle Management system, users can perform CAD data management, change management, BOM management, configuration management, and manufacturing process planning. Users have everything they need to proceed from concept to production, through its service life, eventually to obsolescence.

As development cycles get shorter, with companies wanting to get to market faster, something has to give. That often ends up being training and skills development; so users end up being asked to do more, with less investment in them personally.

This book is written primarily for Creo Parametric users who are new to CAD, and new users coming from another software package. When users are lucky enough to attend training classes or go through adoption programs, the focus tends to be on "picks and clicks" and "features and functions". However, it's important to address why we make those clicks, how we make decisions in our approach to design, and what allows us to make smart models that will adapt to change.

When a person is learning a skill, he or she works towards competence which is knowing what the commands are and how to use them. Then as you move towards proficiency, you begin to grasp *why* you make the choices you do. Finally, as you gain mastery of the skill, you understand the interaction between the design tool, the operator, the product, and the process. Developing an understanding of Design Intent is crucial in this journey towards expertise in Creo Parametric.

Additional Resources

A note on what this book does not contain: this is not an introduction to Creo Parametric. This is not a "picks and clicks" book, although at times it does cover processes and workflows for certain commands. If you are looking for that kind of reference, check out the following sources:

- There are numerous excellent beginner and advanced books on Amazon.com. (Full disclosure: I am a former Amazon employee.)
- PTC offers Instructor-Led Training (ILT), the best way to learn Creo Parametric.
- PTC offers self-paced training at extremely affordable prices through Precision LMS. An annual subscription to the entire Creo Parametric learning library costs less than one day of training.
- Inside Creo Parametric, this is the Learning Connector for immediate on-the-job training in the form of short videos and tutorials.
- The PTC Learning Exchange also offers great how-to videos on a variety of modeling subjects.

Change is a recurring theme throughout this book. Change can be scary. But above all, I strongly recommend that you approach Creo Parametric and the concept of Design Intent with an open mind.

> "Progress is impossible without change, and those who cannot change their minds cannot change anything."
>
> George Bernard Shaw

Version Note

This book was completed in July 2020, almost three years after publication of the first edition. The commands and illustrations depict Creo Parametric 7.0.

Changes from the First Edition

This edition contains additional content compared to the first edition in the following areas:

- Chapter 3 added a section on Design Intent for Additive Manufacturing.
- Chapter 5 on building Design Intent in mechanisms was added.
- Chapter 6 on building Design Intent with Multibody Modeling was added and is relevant in Creo Parametric 7.0 and later.
- Chapter 7 on building Design Intent with engineering calculations was added.
- A section on "More Important Than Design Intent" was added, based on a blog post I wrote for PTC. By the way, publication of the first edition of this book led to me writing for PTC's CAD Thought Leadership and Mathcad blogs.
- An appendix on acronyms was added.

Comments and Feedback

Let me know what you think of this book. I'd love to hear your comments and suggestions, especially regarding how I can make it more helpful and useful in future editions. Feel free to reach out to me at dmartin@creowindchill.com or http://www.creowindchill.com.

1. Introduction to Design Intent

Key Points:

- Since we spend most of our time updating and making changes to our models, we want to build additional information and intelligence into our models so that when we make changes, our models update in ways that we planned for and expect. This is Design Intent.
- Design Intent makes our models parametric, flexible, and robust.
- We can build Design Intent in our sketches, parts, and assemblies.
- There are additional considerations for Design Intent when it comes to mechanisms, Multibody Modeling, engineering calculations, and designing for product variation.

1.1. The Impact of Change

Let us define what exactly we mean by this phrase Design Intent. At the most basic level, it means "what I intend my designs to do." (Shocking, right?) But when it comes to Creo Parametric, Design Intent means a whole lot more. Before we can talk about what that means, we need to discuss the role of change in the product development process.

Most engineers and designers have seen the chart that shows the cost associated with implementing changes over the course of the product development process. It looks like Figure 1-1.

When you start out in the Concept phase, changes you make are inexpensive and comparatively easy to implement. As the design matures, the changes take more time, because changing one thing impacts other components. Handling these impacts takes time, and time does equal money in the business world.

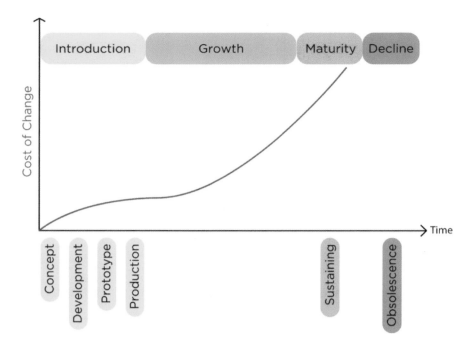

Figure 1-1. Engineering cost vs. time.

After some, most, or all the initial design has taken place, we will start building prototypes. Designing in CAD or on paper is one thing; having a real life, physical object you can touch and examine from every angle is another. (For an example of this see the Stonehenge scene in "This Is Spinal Tap"). Also, simulation and analysis can provide levels of design verification and optimization, but they are no substitute for testing. Simulation and analysis confirm that we are performing the right tests. The point of the prototype is to confirm assumptions, answer questions, and identify areas for improvement.

The prototype phase almost always results in more changes. Even with additive manufacturing, sculpting, mock-ups, or other simplified methods of production, changes now impact materials and labor at a minimum.

Once we're into production, the design changes become significant to manufacturing. Changes to the product mean that we have to modify tooling or scrap existing tooling altogether. We may have to engage new suppliers for materials and components. Production facilities and workflows have to be updated.

Once our product is "out in the field," changes become astronomical. Think of the Ford automotive recall of 21 million vehicles in 1981, or the Samsung Galaxy Note 7 recall of

2 million phones. Engineering changes at this point involve sales, marketing, service departments, and possibly even legal. Your company's reputation could incur permanent damage, and your company might not even survive.

The bottom line is that change happens, and implementing change becomes more burdensome as time passes. Eliminating change isn't an option. All components, assemblies, and products are modified all through their lifespan. We must accept that change happens. We might not like it, but we have to learn to live with it.

With Creo Parametric, we recognize that the initial design phase is only a small portion of the life cycle of a product. You could spend a few hours, maybe a few days, or even a few weeks working on the first iteration of a new part or assembly. But you can spend months, years, or even decades updating and maintaining designs. For example, PTC's first customer John Deere makes construction equipment that can last decades with proper maintenance. I'm sure they are still maintaining CAD models that were originally created in the 1980s.

Therefore, you spend more time modifying a part or assembly than you do designing it initially. The model will go through multiple iterations, and likely multiple revisions. (Life cycle states track the maturity of an object, from birth through death. Examples of life cycle states include Concept, In Work, Released, Production, Sustaining, and Obsolete. Every time an object goes from manufacturing back to engineering, it must be revised.)

Change is constant in the product development process, and engineering is the process of implementing change.

This leads us to the next topic.

1.2. The Definition of Design Intent

Given that we spend more time updating and modifying our design models, we want to build critical information and intelligence into our models, so that when we change one feature, part, or assembly, the other features, parts, and assemblies in our product would also update in ways that we plan and expect. This is Design Intent.

How we build Design Intent in our models is the subject of this book.

What does it mean for our models to have Design Intent?

Our models are parametric: This means when we want to make a change, our models already have the right dimensions and parameters available to make those changes. We do not have to scrap our model and start over because a requirement or critical factor changed.

When we change a feature or component, those changes also affect other features and components in the way that we want them to. For example,

- If the plate size changes, the mounting holes move accordingly.
- If the diameter of those mounting holes changes, the corresponding holes in other parts update automatically.
- If the plate thickness changes, fastener lengths update.

We want to avoid or minimize the number of manual changes we have to implement when other entities change.

Our models are flexible: Change is a fundamental aspect of engineering and product development (If as a person you are not good at adapting to change, then you may have chosen the wrong career). We never know all the requirements up front. The requirements may get "descoped", or they may grow. The goals evolve. We want models that can be updated as these requirements change. We should be able to modify our existing models easily *and not have to start over from scratch with new models*.

Our models are robust: Sometimes changing one entity causes other features or components to fail. When features and components fail in our model, we must invest time and effort fixing those failures. We could spend that time designing new products or optimizing existing ones. Regeneration failures impact our schedule.

It would be great to live in a world where changes never caused features or components to fail. Unfortunately, we do not live in that world. But by building Design Intent in our models, we can significantly reduce the chance that our models will fail.

1.3.   And Away We Go!

The goal of Design Intent is to create parametric, flexible, and robust models that update in ways we plan and expect when we implement changes. In the following chapters we will examine the tools and techniques used to build it into our models at the following levels:

- Sketches
- Parts
- Assemblies

In each chapter, we will cover the techniques for building Design Intent at each level; how we can end up defeating Design Intent with our choices; and a summary of the lessons from that chapter.

In addition, we will look at the impact of Design Intent for Mechanisms, Multibody Modeling, and Engineering Calculations, as well as planning for product variations.

2. Building Design Intent in Sketches

Key Points:

- We build Design Intent into our sketches with our choice of Sketch Plane, Orientation Reference Plane, Sketch References, and the dimensioning scheme.
- Sketch Regions can be used to define Master Sketches. When used in combination with negative Side 2 depths and offsets from To Reference depths, a single Sketch can be used to control multiple Extrudes and Revolves.

2.1. Importance of Sketches in Part Design

Sketches are critical in part modeling as they typically form the basis of our most important features. Part models generally follow the Pareto principle, in that 20% of the features typically generate 80% of the geometry in a model. For parts composed of native geometry (not imported via STEP, IGES, or some other file), these are typically Sketch-Based Features.

In Standard Mode, Sketch-Based Features include Extrudes, Revolves, Sweeps, Helical Sweeps, Blends, Rotational Blends, Swept Blends, and Ribs. Sketches define the shape, boundaries, and/or trajectories of these features. Surface features such as Boundary Blends and Fill Surfaces make extensive use of Sketches.

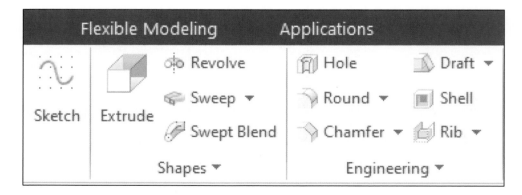

Figure 2-1. Part Mode dashboard showing Sketch and Sketch-Based Features.

In Sheetmetal Mode, Sketches are used to create Primary Walls such as Planar Walls and Extruded Walls. Secondary Walls such as Flat Walls and Flange Walls have standard shapes but can be based on Sketches. Forms can also be based on Sketches.

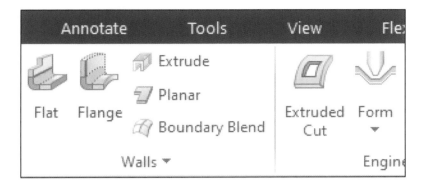

Figure 2-2. Sheetmetal Mode dashboard with tools that can use sketches.

Sketches, therefore, are important in part modeling; when designing or updating part models, you will spend a significant portion of your time in Sketch Mode.

We build Design Intent into our Sketches using the following methods:

- The Sketch Setup (the choice of Sketch Plane and Orientation Reference Plane).
- Sketch References.
- The Dimensioning Scheme (the Constraints and Dimensions).

2.2. Sketch Setup

2.2.1. Sketch Plane

To define a Sketch, we first select the Sketch Plane (the flat planar surface or datum plane) that we want to locate the Sketch on, and generally where we want a subsequent feature to start.

Creo Parametric 4.0 introduced negative secondary depths for Extrude and Revolve features. This means that Extrudes and Revolves no longer need to start from the Sketch Plane. This reduces the need to create Datum Planes, makes design modifications simpler, and builds Design Intent.

In Creo Parametric 3.0 and earlier, if we wanted our feature to start from a different

location, we had to use Edit Definition 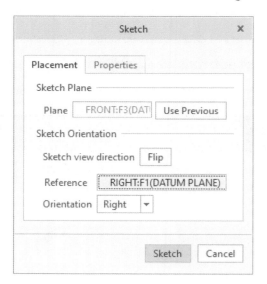 or Edit References . Sometimes that meant creating a Datum Plane at the new location if no reference was available. This enhancement increases flexibility for design change, speeds up workflow, and reduces the need to create additional datum references.

Selecting a flat planar surface or Datum Plane and clicking the Sketch ⎡Sketch⎤ icon puts you immediately into Sketch Mode.

Alternatively, you can click the Sketch ⎡Sketch⎤ icon, select your Sketch Plane, and then click OK to enter Sketch Mode. The Sketch definition dialog box looks as follows:

Figure 2-3. The Sketch Definition Dialog Box.

2.2.2. Orientation Reference Plane

When defining a Sketch, Creo Parametric selects an Orientation Reference Plane for you. (In the Sketch definition dialog box, this is simply labeled as "Reference," but I prefer calling it the "Orientation Reference Plane" because that describes what it does.)

This Orientation Reference Plane was more important in earlier versions of Pro/ENGINEER (the predecessor to Creo Parametric). In the past, when entering Sketch Mode, the software forced the model to reorient so that:

- The Sketch Plane was parallel to the screen.
- The model was oriented looking at the front or back of the Sketch Plane depending on the viewing direction of the Sketch.
- The Orientation Reference Plane faced the top, bottom, right, or left side of the computer screen.

This would rotate the model when entering Sketch Mode. It confused many users.

The Orientation Reference Plane is not as important anymore for the following reasons:

- The configuration option *sketcher_starts_in_2d* was added, and later its default value was changed to no. The model retains its current orientation when entering Sketch Mode.
- The software will automatically suggest an Orientation Reference Plane and the side of the computer screen for you.
- If Creo cannot suggest an Orientation Reference Plane, it will create an internal reference automatically. This saves you from creating a datum plane simply for the purpose of orienting the model in Sketch Mode.

Although this Orientation Reference Plane isn't as important anymore, it still creates a Parent-Child Relationship between the Sketch and whatever is selected. (Parent-Child Relationships are covered in more detail in Chapter 3.) If that reference changes, then the sketch will update appropriately. If something happens to the reference to remove it from the model, the sketch will fail regeneration.

Therefore, to preserve Design Intent, make sure to:

- Verify that Creo Parametric has selected a good, stable reference for you.
- Only use something as an Orientation Reference Plane that you intend to use as a Sketch Reference later.

Sketch References are covered in the next topic.

2.3.   Sketch References

When you enter Sketch Mode, Creo Parametric automatically selects entities that are used to define dimensions. In simple terms, I like to think of these as the x- and y- axes of the sketch. Often these may be default datum planes or the default coordinate system. These are known as the Sketch References.

Do not blindly accept Creo Parametric's suggestions. Although default datums are the most stable features in your model, they may not reflect the way you want to control your sketch.

One particularly bad sketching technique is extending entities beyond the part geometry to ensure that the sketch fully intersects or cuts through the model. This technique creates additional meaningless dimensions, and the sketch does not update with changes to model geometry.

Instead, add your part's boundaries to your list of Sketch References. Then your sketched entities will lock into model geometry, and update with changes to it.

Along the same lines, locking into model geometry can be powerful when using open sketches. A closed sketch is one that forms a loop; the start and end of the figure are the same. In an open sketch, the entities do not form a loop. By default, Creo Parametric highlights the open ends in red.

- A sketch to be used for a Sketch-Based Feature can contain multiple closed loops.
- A sketch can contain only one open loop.
- A sketch for a Sketch-Based Feature can contain multiple closed loops in addition to a single open loop.

> The Profile Rib feature requires an open Sketch, and it must start and end on part geometry.

Also note the following for how open loops behave: An open loop will either extrapolate or ride along the adjoining surface to which it is attached. This is convenient for filling in gaps or continuing the shape of the adjoining surface. For example, here is an open sketch on a conical surface:

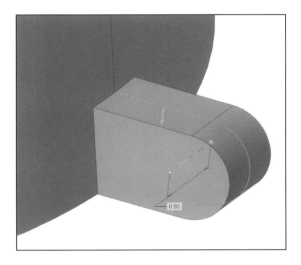

Figure 2-4: Open sketch behavior.

When the same sketch is closed, you can see gaps between the conical surface and the new extrude:

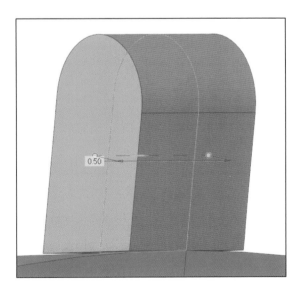

Figure 2-5: Closed sketch behavior.

A few guidelines regarding Sketch References:

- The Sketch References dialog box can be accessed by holding down the right mouse button and selecting References (when nothing is selected). The References command is also available from the Setup group in the Ribbon.

Figure 2-6. The Sketch References Dialog Box.

- Use the <ALT> key to create Sketch References on the fly.
- Surfaces are better Sketch References than edges since they are more stable.
- Creating constraints and dimensions to model geometry will automatically add those entities to your list of Sketch References.
- The Sketch References you select that you don't actually use will automatically be removed from the list of Sketch References when you exit Sketch Mode.

2.4.   Dimensioning Scheme

The dimensioning scheme of a sketch consists of both the dimensions and the constraints. *Dimensions* describe the size of entities and can include values such as length, distance, radius, diameter, angles, and perimeter. *Constraints* are rules placed on your sketch entities. These include vertical, horizontal, parallel, perpendicular, tangent, symmetric, equal, mid-point, and coincident.

2.4.1. Sketcher Constraints

While sketching, Creo Parametric suggests constraints to the user. The available constraints are available in the Ribbon as shown in Figure 2-5.

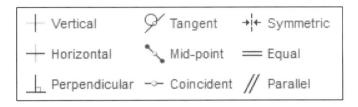

Figure 2-7. Sketcher Constraints from the Ribbon.

Constraints build Design Intent because they determine how the entities change when the rest of the sketch updates.

While sketching you can use the following additional controls:

- Tapping the right mouse button will allow you to cycle between enabling, disabling, and locking in the constraints that appear. The constraint is locked in when a circle appears around it.
- If multiple constraints are displayed, hitting the <TAB> key on the keyboard allows you to change which one is active. You can click the right mouse button to enable, disable, and lock affects the active constraint.
- Holding down the <SHIFT> key prevents Creo from suggesting constraints.

Recommendation: add constraints prior to creating new dimensions. As constraints are added, weak dimensions are removed.

2.4.2. Dimensions

After sketching entities, Creo Parametric automatically suggests the necessary dimensions to control the size of the geometric entities. These suggested dimensions are known as weak dimensions. It is a healthy practice to make sure that all your dimensions are strong before leaving Sketch Mode.

To create strong dimensions instead of weak dimensions, perform any of the following actions:

- Double click on a weak dimension and change its value.
- Select one or more dimensions, and use CTRL-T, the Strong command from the Mini Toolbar, or Operations > Convert To > Strong.

Figure 2-8: Mini Toolbar for Dimensions.

- Create a new dimension: New dimensions are always strong and will remove weak dimensions from the model.

The general technique used for dimensioning is as follows:

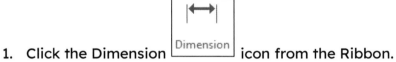

1. Click the Dimension icon from the Ribbon.
2. Pick what you want to dimension with the left mouse button. This may be a one or more entities depending on the type of dimension.
3. Move your mouse where you want the dimension to appear and click the middle mouse button to locate the dimension.
4. Type in a value for the dimension or hit <ENTER> to accept the current value.

Consider the following when choosing a dimensioning scheme:

- If you pick the endpoints of a line, you are controlling a distance. If you pick the line itself, you are controlling a length. There is a difference.
- Weak diameter dimensions are created for circles, and weak radius dimensions are created for arcs. You can select the weak dimension and the Convert to Radius, Convert to Diameter, or Convert to Linear tool from the Mini Toolbar as appropriate.

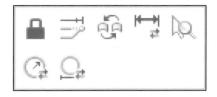 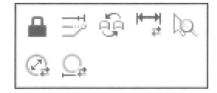

Figure 2-9: Mini Toolbars for Circles and Arcs.

- Ordinate dimensions can also be created. First, use the [⊟ Baseline] icon to define your zero. Then click the Dimension [|↔| Dimension] icon; hold down the <CTRL> key; select the baseline and the entities you want to dimension to it, and middle click to locate the dimensions.

- The direction of a distance dimension is from the first entity to the second entity; in obscure situations, this can make a difference.

- Dimensions can be locked so that dragging entities in Sketch Mode or Part Mode will not change their values. To lock a dimension, select it and choose Lock from the Mini Toolbar. The configuration option *sketcher_dimension_autolock* can be set to yes to lock all manually created dimensions.

In addition to standard length, distance, radius, diameter, and other normal kinds of dimensions, the following advanced dimensions can also be created:

- Reference dimensions: The configuration option *parenthesize_ref_dim* controls whether it appears in parentheses or with REF after it.

- Diameter dimensions for revolved features.

- Arc length and arc angles dimensions. If you accidentally create the wrong type, you can select the dimension and choose Convert to Angle or Convert to Length tool from the Mini Toolbar.

Figure 2-10: Mini Toolbar for an arc length dimension.

- Total included angles for mirrored geometry.

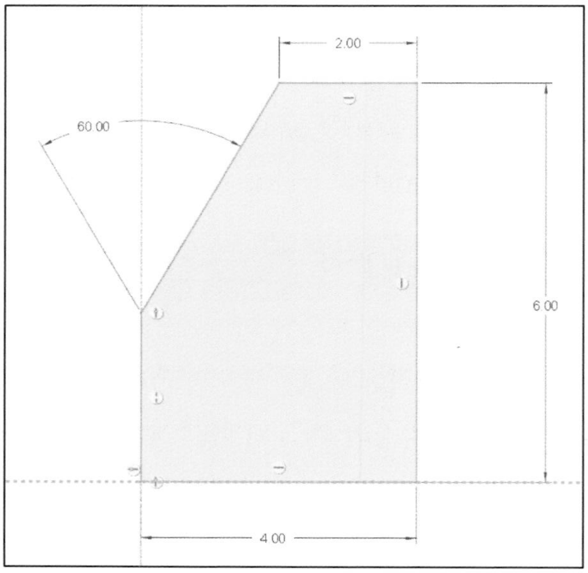

Figure 2-11. Total included angle dimension.

- Tangency angle dimensions for splines and conics, and Radius of curvature dimensions for splines.
- Perimeter dimensions.

The old rule of thumb was that 95% of the dimensions shown on a drawing should come from the model. As discussed in section 3.8.2.3, this is no longer true due to the advent of Model Based Definition (MBD) and Flexible Modeling.

2.5. Sketch Regions

In Creo Parametric 5.0, Sketch Regions were introduced. This enables users to create sketch-based features like Extrudes or Revolves using one or more enclosed areas of a Sketch. For this reason, the old restrictions on overlapping loops from Creo Parametric 4.0 and earlier no longer applies.

Users should take this into account when planning their part models. You can use one or more "Master Sketches" that contains the majority of the defining geometry for a given plane.

These Sketch Regions and Master Sketches can be used in conjunction with the following depth enhancements for Extrudes introduced in Creo Parametric 4.0:

- Negative depths for Side 2, so that the Extrude no longer has to start from the Sketch Plane. The depths for Side 1 and Side 2 can be on the same side of the Sketch Plane.
- To Selected depth options that are offset from the selected reference. The offset distance can be measured:
  - Parallel to the selected depth reference.
  - Parallel to the Sketch Plane.

Any Extrudes, Revolves, or Fill features based off a Sketch Region contain internal sketches that have Sketch References to the original Sketch Region. Therefore, changes to the original Sketch feature used for the Sketch Regions can require the Sketch References to be updated or can cause regeneration failures in the internal sketches.

The following figure shows an example of 5 Extrude features created in the same part using a variety of depth options:

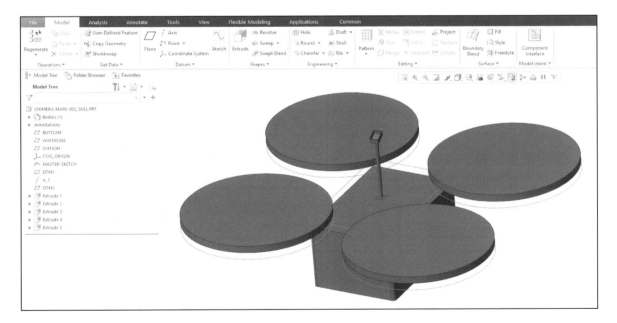

Figure 2-12: Geometry created from a Master Sketch.

The combination of Sketch Regions and depth options vastly expands the capability to build Design Intent into sketch-based features.

2.6. How Design Intent Gets Defeated

Let us discuss the ways in which users work against Design Intent for Sketches. As users, we may gravitate towards the methods that are quickest and easiest. Design Intent is not about how fast you can build a model. It's about building the model in such a way that it can be modified twenty, thirty, forty, or more times, and building models and features that update properly when other entities change.

Here are some of the ways in which Design Intent gets defeated in Sketches:

Overly complicated sketches: Some users think that a shorter Model Tree makes a better model, so they pack as many entities as they can into a single sketch. This is not the case. Overly complicated sketches, as in Figure 2-7, make models harder to update and maintain.

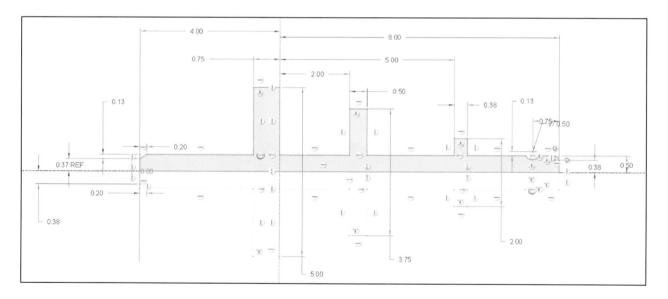

Figure 2-13. Overcomplicated sketch with numerous bad techniques.

Lesson: more features make a model easier to maintain.

Putting rounds and chamfers in the sketch: This is closely related to having too many geometric entities in the Sketch. (Also shown in Figure 2-8.)

Lesson: rounds and chamfers should be created in their own features.

Duplicating features in a sketch: Rather than use part modeling tools such as Patterns, Copy and Paste, and Mirror, users overload the sketch by placing the multiple closed-loop entities in the sketch. Refer to Figure 2-8. How could the mounting schemes be accomplished with Patterns instead?

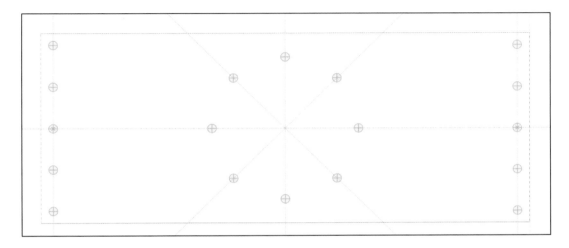

Figure 2-14. Two different mounting patterns captured in the same sketch.

Lesson: use Feature Duplication tools like Pattern and Mirror instead of creating entities in the Sketch.

Not using Sketch References to lock into part geometry: Some users think that to ensure that a cut fully slices through a model they should extend the sketch geometry beyond the model's borders. Refer to Figure 2-10; which dimension has no meaning? (Answer: the 20 dimension.)

Lesson: use Sketch References to lock into model geometry.

Using the wrong dimensioning scheme: Sometimes when sketching, Creo might suggest a radius dimension for a hole. However, that hole will most likely be drilled and then inspected using a diameter dimension.

Lesson: use the correct dimensioning scheme based on what you are trying to control from a manufacturing, inspection, and tolerances perspective.

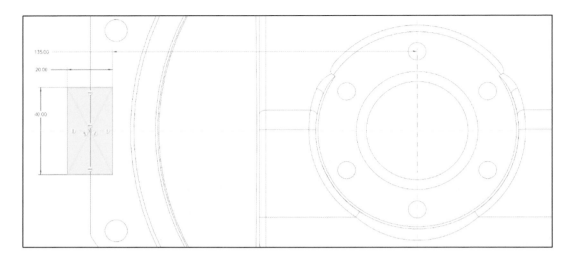

Figure 2-15: Sketch for a cut extending past part geometry.

Using bad dimensioning schemes: Bad dimensioning schemes are either exceeding difficult or impossible to measure. For example:

- Dimensioning to the tangent edge between a flat and rounded surface.
- Dimensions to "outer space" or worse, reference geometry from another component.
- Dimensions to the top-level assembly's origin.

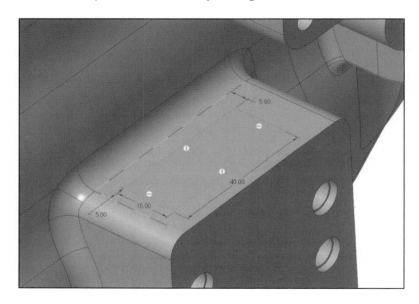

Figure 2-16. Sketch with dimensions to tangent edges.

Relations in Sketches: Relations are covered in Chapter 3, but they are mentioned here to explain why they should be avoided in Sketches. Relations are equations and mathematical expressions that we write in our models to control parameters and dimensions by other parameters and dimensions, scalar values, or some evaluated result.

Although Relations can be written at the Sketch level, this practice should be avoided.

First, it is not obvious to other users at all that a Sketch has Relations. A user has to look for them deliberately to become aware of their existence, and that can lead to confusion and frustration. Model > Model Intent > Relations and Parameters is one of the few tools that allows the user to find Relations at the Sketch level.

Secondly, Relations written at the Part level are evaluated at the beginning of the regeneration cycle before the features are regenerated. Relations in Sketches are evaluated when the Sketch is regenerated. Because of this, the part:

- Requires more than one regeneration to ensure all dimensions and parameters are up to date.
- May retrieve with a yellow regeneration status.
- May have a permanent yellow regeneration status.

Models should retrieve with a green regeneration status and should only require one regeneration cycle to update all dimensions, parameters, and geometry.

2.7. Summary

To build and maintain Design Intent in Sketches you should follow these practices:

- Choose Sketch Planes carefully.
- Select an Orientation Reference Plane that you intend to use as a Sketch Reference.
- Select the Sketch References that help you implement your Design Intent. Use model boundaries as Sketch References so your sketch entities can snap to them.
- The dimensioning scheme consists of both constraints and dimensions.

- Constraints are rules placed on the geometry in your sketch. Adding constraints removes weak dimensions from your sketch.
- The dimensions should reflect how you want to control the geometry and how you intend to measure and inspect your part later.

- The dimensions in your sketch should be the ones you will use in the production drawing.
- Do not leave any weak dimension in your sketch.

3. Building Design Intent in Parts

Key Points

- There are numerous ways of building Design Intent at the part level, including choice of features, feature options, parent-child relationships, order of features, Relations, and the Behavioral Modeling Extension (BMX).
- Other considerations for Design Intent at the part level include surfacing, combining direct modeling with parametric modeling, and design for Additive Manufacturing.

3.1.   Part Modeling Overview

A part is a model that:

- consists of features and typically represents an object made out of a single material or composite material;
- is manufactured under a defined set of processes; and,
- is controlled as a distinct, discrete unit.

However, this is a loose definition.

- Assemblies can be modeled in Creo Parametric as a part file.
- Starting in Creo Parametric 7.0, Multibody Modeling is available. Bodies are distinct volumes that can have different material assignments.
- In Windchill, the term "Part" is used to describe both parts and assemblies modeled in Creo Parametric.

Strictly speaking, a part in Creo Parametric is a model consisting of features that is stored with a .prt file extension.

We build Design Intent into Part models primarily through the following methods:

- Feature Choice.
- Feature Options.

- Parent-Child Relationships.
- Feature Order.
- Relations.
- Behavioral Modeling.

In addition to these methods of building Design Intent we will examine other considerations, including:

- More artistic methods of creating Industrial Design (ID) geometry, such as Freeform Surfacing and Subdivisional Modeling.
- The Direct Modeling Paradigm and how it can be combined with traditional parametric modeling in Creo Parametric.

3.2.   Feature Choice

We have numerous different classes of features that we can create in part models, and these different classes contain multiple different types of features. You will often have multiple choices that will create the same result. Which is the best choice?

- The first method that comes to mind?
- The easiest method?
- The fastest one?
- The one that requires the fewest mouse clicks?

If you chose any of the above, you might want to start reading this book again from page 1. The best choice depends on Design Intent. Let's look at an example to illustrate this choice:

3.2.1. Why Feature Choice Matters

Consider the following example: how can you make this cylinder?

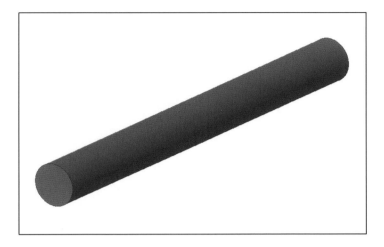

Figure 3-1. A simple cylinder part model.

Some of the more of the obvious methods include:

- Sketch a circle and use the Extrude tool.
- Sketch a rectangle and use the Revolve tool.
- Use the Blend tool to connect two circular sections.
- Sketch a straight line and then use the Sweep tool with a circular profile.

Which of these methods is the best? That is a loaded question. We don't know which method is the best until we consider how our Design Intent can change over time.

Take the following situations into consideration:

- If the cylinder might change into a shape other than circular, then the Extrude would be the best choice in this situation (see the yellow object in Figure 3-2).
- If the angle of revolution might change to something less than 360 degrees, then the Revolve would be our solution (see the blue object in Figure 3-2).
- If the critical factor is controlling the shape at both ends of the geometry, then we would want to choose the Blend (see the green object in Figure 3-2).
- If the path (trajectory) could change, then the Sweep would best allow us to account for this change in Design Intent (see the red object in Figure 3-2).

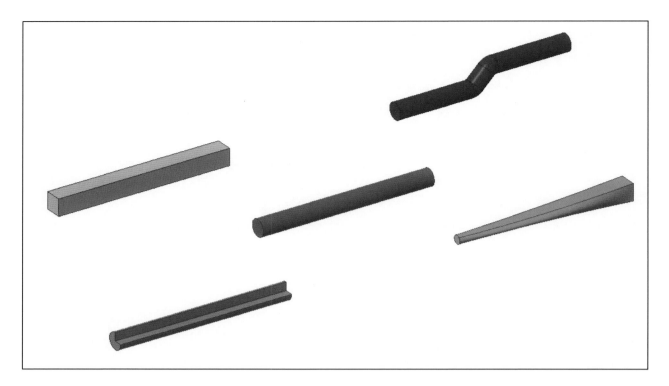

Figure 3-2. Effect of Feature Choice on Design Intent.

Before making a choice, consider the most likely scenarios that might change your requirements later. Let that be your guide when selecting which features to choose.

3.2.2. Classes of Features

There are numerous different classes of features that can be created in part models, including:

- Datum Features: imaginary references that we place in our model to create and control other features in our model.
- Sketch-Based Features: these features add or remove geometry from the model by performing operations on Sketches. Examples include the Extrude and Revolve tools.
- Engineering Features: these are features in which the basic geometry or shape is already defined. The user specifies references to locate the features in the model, dimensions to control the size, and other various options. These include Holes, Rounds, Chamfers, Shells, and Draft.

- Surface Features: these features create a three-dimensional geometry that has no thickness, and therefore no mass. Users can create more organic, ergonomic, and aesthetically pleasing shapes than can be created with traditional Sketch-Based Features. "Technical" or "parametric" surfaces include Boundary Blends and Fill features.
- Editing Features: these take other features or geometry and manipulate them. These include features such as Trim, Extend, and Merge.
- Feature Duplication: these features take one or more features as inputs, and allow the user to create additional features, which may be copies, mirrors, or pattern instances.

This is by far not an exclusive list. Other classes include:

- Data Sharing Features used in Top Down Design, as discussed in section 4.6.3.
- Annotation Features used in Model Based Definition (MBD).
- Flexible Modeling features, as discussed in section 3.8.2.1.

The critical point is that in design, you will often have to make choices regarding which class of feature you want to use. For example, are you going to make your primary features sketch-based or surfaces? And if so, which one of the types of features in that class will you choose?

If you decide to model using surfaces, which technique(s) will you use? These include:

- Parametric (sometimes referred to as technical) surfacing. These features include Boundary Blends, Sweeps, and Swept Blends.
- Freeform surfacing (the Style feature within ISDX, the Interactive Surfacing Design Extension).
- Subdivisional modeling (the Freestyle feature).

Ask yourself these questions when choosing the class and type of feature to build:

- What are my requirements, design constraints, and goals today?
- What information do I have now?
- What information do I need?
- How might my requirements, design constraints, and goals change in the future?

- What features are most likely to accommodate my requirements?
- Which of these choices are most adaptable to change, preferably without resulting in regeneration failures or high amounts of rework? In other words, which of my feature choices are most robust and flexible?

We will quickly review some examples of some of the different kinds of features in the various classes.

3.2.2.1. Datum Features

Datums provide geometric references in your model so that you can define features. Most standard model templates provide three default datum planes and a default coordinate system as a starting point. Datums are also used for documentation in the 1994 ASME standard (Y14.5) for Geometric Dimensioning and Tolerancing (GD&T). Types of Datum Features include:

- Planes [Plane]

- Axes [Axis]

- Points [Point ▼]

- Coordinate Systems [Coordinate System]
- Curves

> By default, an extruded circle and a sketch revolved through 360 degrees and generate axes automatically. Extruded arcs and revolves less than 360 degrees do not create axes. The configuration option *show_axes_for_extr_arcs* will generate axes for both situations.

3.2.2.2. Sketch-Based Features

As discussed in the previous chapter, Sketch-Based features are some of the most widely used features in part models. The base (first solid) feature is often based on a sketch. These include:

- Extrude ⬚Extrude: add or remove material normal to the Sketch.
- Revolve ⬚Revolve: add or remove material about an axis of revolution.
- Sweep ⬚Sweep ▾: move a sketch along the main trajectory. Additional trajectories can be used to control the shape, and the section can be allowed to vary along the main trajectory by a variety of means.
- Blend ⬚Blend: connect multiple sections together to create a feature.

Note that in addition to creating solid geometry, Sketch-Based Features can also create surfaces and quilts (non-solid features).

A Note About Internal Sketches

A Sketch does not need to exist prior to creating an Extrude or a Revolve; it can be created within the feature. This is known as an *Internal Sketch*. When the Sketch is created first it is known as an *External Sketch*.

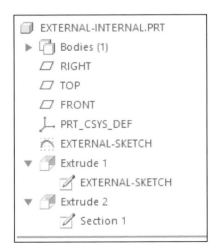

Figure 3-3. External vs. Internal Sketches for features.

External Sketches provide more flexibility because:

- The same sketch can be used to drive multiple features.
- A feature can quickly be changed to use a different External Sketch. With an Internal Sketch, all the entities would need to be deleted and the new sketch created.

An External Sketch can be converted to an Internal Sketch by using the Unlink button in the Placement tab of the Sketch-Based Feature.

Figure 3-4. Unlinking an external sketch from a feature dashboard.

3.2.2.3. Editing Features

Editing features perform operations on existing features and geometry in our model. They include:

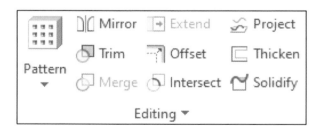

Figure 3-5. Editing features in the part mode ribbon.

- Trim: use one object to reduce the extent of another object.
- Merge: stitch two or more quilts together.
- Extend: increase the boundaries of a surface.
- Offset: create new curves or surfaces of moving a parent entity a specified distance in a specified direction.

- Thicken: create solid geometry by offsetting a surface, creating side surfaces, merging the result, and filling in the interior volume.
- Solidify: create solid geometry, either adding or removing material, using a quilt as an input.

3.2.2.4. Engineering Features

The basic shape of Engineering Features is already defined. These features are placed in the model by specifying location references and attributes regarding size and extent.

Figure 3-6. Feature tools from the Engineering group on the Model tab.

Engineering features include:

- Hole: a circular cut in a model. They include Straight, Standard, and Sketched holes. They can be tapered and have countersinks and/or counterbores.
- Rounds: break a sharp corner with rounded or conic geometry. These are sometimes called fillets.
- Chamfer: remove sharp corners from an object, leaving a flat beveled surface.
- Draft: add taper to the surfaces of a model to facilitate manufacturing via molds and casts.
- Shell: hollow out a part to a given thickness, optionally removing specified surfaces to provide access to the interior volume.

Holes vs. Extrudes

Holes present an interesting choice when it comes to Design Intent. A simple hole can be created by simply extruding a circle as a cut. If the hole could likely change to a slot, then an Extrude would be preferred. But otherwise, hole features provide numerous advantages, including:

- Changing between different dimensioning schemes.
- Easily adding counterbores, countersinks, and exit countersinks.
- Selecting standard holes from preconfigured lists for tapped, clearance, and tapered holes. These can include thread surfaces and automatically generated notes to be used in drawings.
- Reducing regeneration time with lightweight holes.
- Searching for holes and placing them with layers for suppression of downstream processes.

3.2.2.5. Declaration Features

This class of features do not affect the part's topology and only reference the final geometry. For this reason, these features can appear in the Footer folder at the bottom of the Model Tree. These include:

- Zones: a method of selecting multiple components in an assembly for applying different actions from Simplified Representations. This was necessary prior to box selection methods being added. Zones can also be used to create 3D cross sections in parts and assemblies.
- Publish Geometry features: these are used in Top Down Design (TDD) to consolidate geometry references that another model might need to use as External References.
- Annotations used as part of Model Based Definition (MBD).
- Datum Reference Features: these little-used features are used to create Intent Objects consisting of surfaces, edges, curves, points, and other datum features. These Datum Reference Features can then be used as Intent References when creating features such as Rounds, Chamfers, and Draft.
- Component Interfaces: these define how a component can be placed in an assembly and how components can be assembled to it. These are time savers for components that are routinely placed using the same methods.

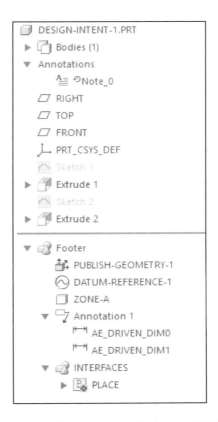

Figure 3-7: Declaration Features in the Model Tree Footer.

3.2.3. Duplication Methods

The power of computers lies in their ability to iterate, to perform operations over and over, faster than we can, saving us the time and effort of doing things manually. Creo Parametric takes the same approach with duplicating features, using the following tools:

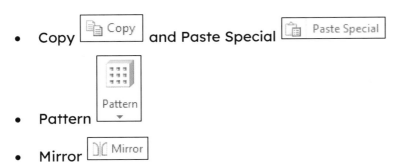

- Copy and Paste Special
- Pattern
- Mirror

Duplicating features using these methods provide greater control and Design Intent than creating multiple entities in a Sketch (which is a bad practice).

3.2.3.1. Copy and Paste Special

While Copy and Paste saves you from recreating features, it does not build Design Intent in the model because there is no dependency between the original object(s) and the copies. However, Paste Special does allow dependency; a Parent-Child Relationship can be established so that changes to the original are propagated to the duplicate.

However, if it has been a while since you last used this command, practice on some sample models first. There are nuances to the command that are not intuitive.

To perform this operation, do the following:

1. Select the feature(s) you wish to copy.

2. Use CTRL-C or the Copy [Copy] command.

3. Click the Paste drop-down menu (just below the Copy command in the Operations group on the Model tab) and select the Paste Special [Paste Special] command.

Here is where things get tricky. The Paste Special dialog box will open:

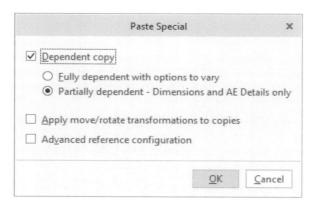

Figure 3-8. The Paste Special dialog box.

By default, Dependent copy and Partially dependent - Dimensions and AE Details only are selected. Some notes about this first option:

• It may be necessary to use this in conjunction with Advanced reference configuration to locate the copy in a new place.

- If you attempt to edit the definition of the sketch for a copied Sketch-Based Feature, you will receive a warning:

Figure 3-9. Warning for editing definition of a dependent sketch.

- If you right click on a copied Sketch-Based Feature, the command Copied Feature > Make Section Independent is available to break the Parent-Child Relationship.

- If you attempt to edit certain dimensions in the copy, you will see this warning:

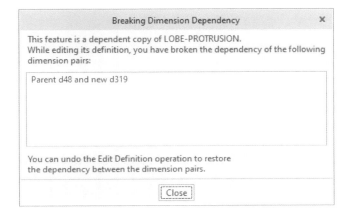

Figure 3-10. Break dimension dependency warning.

Here are some notes regarding the Fully dependent with options to vary choice:

- The copied feature(s) will have the word "Copied" at the start of its name in the Model Tree.
- Edit Definition is not available for these features.

- Any options that are varied can be viewed in the Varied Items table:

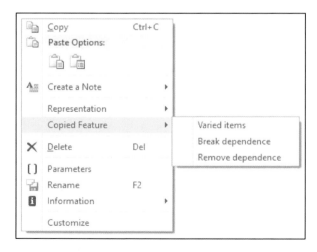

Figure 3-11. Copied feature Varied Items dialog box.

- Right clicking on the copied feature(s) will provide access to the Copied Feature commands to access the Varied Items table and control the dependency (see Figure 3-11).
  - Break dependence temporarily suspends the duplicate from updating with changes to the original.
  - Restore dependence re-establishes a broken dependency.
  - Remove dependence permanently stops changes from being propagated.

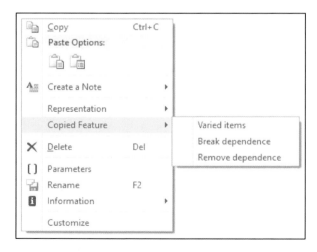

Figure 3-12. Copied Feature right mouse button commands.

Familiarize yourself with the repercussions of the various options before using the command to be aware of limitations to future changes.

3.2.3.2. Patterns

Patterns allow us to create multiple instances of a feature, or a group of features, using a variety of methods:

- Dimension: define increments for the dimensions used to define the feature(s).
- Direction: create patterns in one or two directions by translation, rotation, coordinate systems, or a mix of these.
- Axis: create a rotational pattern in one or two directions.
- Fill: use an open or closed curve as either a boundary or a trajectory for locating instances.
- Table: fill in a spreadsheet for values to define the instance's location and size.
- Reference: use an existing pattern as the basis for creating a new pattern. More on this below.
- Curve: create a pattern by following a defined path.
- Point: use a Sketch or Datum Point array to define the location of instances. This is much quicker and easier than a Table Pattern.

> Tip: Point Patterns can use Sketcher Coordinate Systems in addition to Points. This is very convenient for modeling cabling connector entry ports and placing forms in Sheetmetal parts.

By default, under the most basic circumstances, all the instances will be created identically to the lead feature of the pattern. In this way, we build Design Intent because changes to the lead feature(s) are propagated to the pattern instances.

However, we can get the instances to vary using a number of techniques:

- The dimensions describing the shape of the feature could be incremented. This increment can be defined using a Relation. This applies to Dimension, Direction, and Axis Patterns.

- The pattern uses a table that includes feature dimensions in addition to locating dimensions.
- The patterned features could have Sketch References, depth options, or some other Parent-Child Relationship that cause them to vary.

Figure 3-13: Sketch References used to change instances in a Dimension Pattern.

Reference Patterns

The Reference Pattern is a particularly strong method of building Design Intent into models via feature duplication. If the original pattern changes, then the pattern that references it automatically updates.

This is even stronger at the assembly level. Let's say we have a pattern of holes in a part. Then we have a series of components assembled to those holes, such as a vibration mount, washers, screws, and nuts. If the pattern of holes changes (we increase or decrease the number of instances or change the spacing between the holes) all the components will update automatically. Additional components will be added or removed if necessary, and the locations updated. This is the essence of Design Intent: our models update when changes happen, exactly as we expect them to, without us having to do anything.

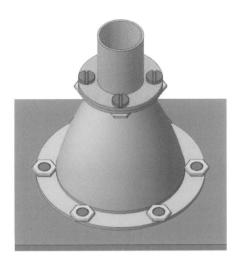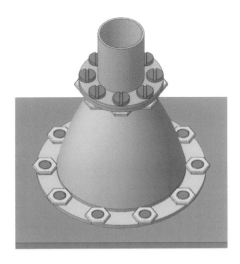

Figure 3-14: Reference pattern updating.

3.2.3.3. Mirror

If our model has one, two, or even three planes of symmetry, we can use this to our advantage by modeling only half, a quarter, or an eighth of our part, and then create one, two, or three Mirror features.

With this technique, the mirrors are always dependent on the original portion, so if you modify a feature, those changes are propagated to the mirrored portions. The process of doing this is as follows:

1. Select the top node in the Model Tree (the line with <model_name>.PRT).
2. Select the Mirror ⬚⬚ Mirror command.
3. Select the plane or surface you want to mirror about.
4. Click the middle mouse button to complete the feature.

One or more features in the model can also be mirrored, following the same general procedure. By default, it is set to Dependent using the Partially dependent; Dimensions and AE Details only option. These settings can be changed from the Options tab in the dashboard:

Figure 3-15. Dependency for a mirrored feature.

See Section 3.1.3.1 on Copy and Paste Special for more information regarding the dependency options.

3.3.   Feature Options

The dashboard used to create various features contains numerous additional attributes and options that can be specified to define your feature. There are too many features to cover all the options, but we will discuss some examples.

3.3.1.   Depth and Angle Options

The typical depth options for an Extrude or a Hole are:

- Blind: a numerical value is entered.
- Symmetric: a numerical value is entered, but half the depth is applied on each side of the Sketch Plane.
- To Next: the feature extends until it intersects the very next surface.
- Through All: the feature goes through all geometry that exists in the model. This option is appropriate for removing material only.
- Through Until.
- To Selected.

The angles for a Revolve feature include:

- Variable: a numerical value is entered.
- Symmetric.
- To Selected.

Blind, Symmetric, and Variable are based on numbers. Unless those values are controlled by Relations (more on those later in this chapter), they don't update for changes made to the model.

The other options can update the resulting feature with changes made to their references or geometry prior to them in the model. For example:

- If geometry appears in the path of an Extrude or a Hole set to To Next, the feature will terminate.
- If geometry appears above the feature in the Model Tree and in the path of an Extrude or a Hole set to Through All, it will be intersected.
- If the reference chosen for Through Until or To Selected moves, then the Extrude or Hole will update its depth, and a Revolve will update its angle.

Depth and angle options build Design Intent into our models.

A Note About To Selected vs. Through Until

These depth options fundamentally do the same thing. However, Through Until has a critical distinction: the feature must fully intersect the reference selected. If that reference gets changed such that the feature no longer fully intersects it, the feature will fail.

Therefore, To Selected is a much more robust option when compared to Through Until. To Selected should always be used instead of Through Until (unless you would want a potential regeneration failure triggered by a change to the reference, but I cannot fathom a situation like that).

3.3.2. Other Examples

All features have various options that can be selected during creation and Edit Definition. If you are a new user, take a minute or two to read the various choices in the dashboard, Mini Toolbars, and right mouse button menu.

We will take a look at some options for a few features. Think about how those choices will result in the feature reacting to change.

Rounds

- Is the radius driven by a curve or a point / vertex?
- Is it a full round where the removed surface determines the size of the feature?
- Constant or variable radius. For variable radius rounds, are you locating the radius handles using length ratio or a point / vertex?

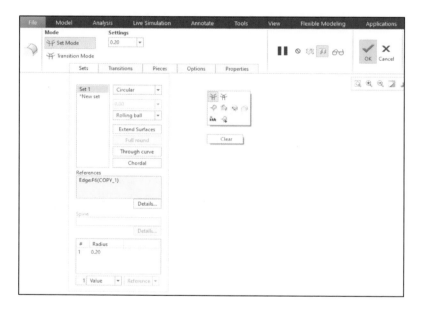

Figure 3-16: The Rounds dashboard and Mini Toolbar.

Draft

- What object are you using as the Draft Hinge?
- If you are splitting the Draft? What are you using to split it?
- Are you using variable draft angles? If so, are you locating the handles using length ratio or a point / vertex?

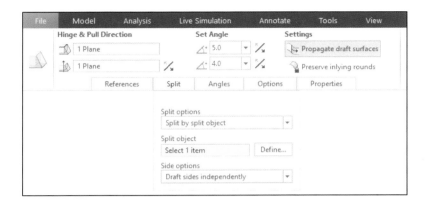

Figure 3-17: The Draft dashboard and Split tab.

Shells

- Are you applying a non-default thickness to any surfaces?
- Are you excluding any surfaces from the Shell feature?

Figure 3-18: The Shell feature and References tab.

Patterns

- Can you change from a General Pattern to Identical or Varying for better regeneration performance, or will the pattern become more likely to fail?
- For Curve Patterns, do you want to control the spacing or the total number of instances?
- For Fill, Point, and Curve Patterns, do you want the instances to follow the shape of some other surface?

Your model's Design Intent is determined by all the choices you make, especially those that tie your feature to other features. This leads us right into our next section.

3.4. Feature References: Parent-Child Relationships

Parent-Child Relationships have been mentioned a few times before in this book. They are critical because they determine how our models are parametric, how changes are propagated from one feature to other features.

Parent-Child Relationships in Creo Parametric work in the following manner:

- Whenever you create a new feature, you have to select existing features in the model as references, in order to determine things like location, shape, and size.
- The new feature you are creating will be the child of the existing feature.
- The existing feature will be the parent of the new feature.
- In Creo Parametric, children are absolutely dependent on their parents. Changes to the parents will be propagated to the children. And if you want to delete or suppress a parent, by default, Creo Parametric will want to delete or suppress the child.

Parent-Child Relationships are also created in assemblies. When we assemble a new component to an existing component, that new component is the child and the existing component is the parent. Parent-Child Relationships can also be created in assemblies via External References, which will be discussed in Section 4.4.

Table 3-1 contains examples of Parent-Child Relationships that are created during feature creation.

Table 3-1. *Parent-Child Relationships*

Feature Class	Feature	References
Datum	Planes and Axes	Location references, display size reference
	Coordinate System	Origin location reference, axes direction references
Sketch	Sketch	Sketch Plane, Orientation Reference Plane, Sketch References
Sketch-Based	Extrude	Sketch, Depth Options
	Revolve	Sketch, Angle Options
	Sweeps	Trajectories, section plane control reference, x-vector / direction references, sketch placement point
	Blends	Sketches, boundary condition references
	Ribs	Sketch
Engineering	Rounds	Edges and surfaces to define placement; curves, vertices, and points to define radius
	Chamfers	Edges, surfaces, and corners to define placement
	Holes	Placement surfaces, location references, depth options
	Shells	Surfaces to be removed, excluded surfaces, and non-default thickness surfaces
	Draft	Draft surfaces, draft hinge, pull direction, split references
Editing	Mirror	Objects to be mirrored, mirror plane
	Trim	Quilts, trimming object (curve, quilt, plane)
	Merge	Quilts

Given that Parent-Child Relationships build Design Intent, how do we use them to build better models?

- Choose references carefully. The more stable they are, the better. By stable, that means they are either not likely to change or will change in very predictable ways that are not disruptive.
- The fewer the references, the better.
- Surfaces are better choices than edges.
- Use Advanced Selection Methods or Intent References (see below) if you can.
- Default datum planes are the most stable features in your model. They can make great parents. However, go with the logical choice for how you want changes to be propagated in your model.

3.4.1. Location of First Feature

One of the most important references for a part model is the location of the first solid feature. If your model has symmetry, do you sketch it to be symmetric about one of your Default Datum Planes? This can facilitate mirroring features later because you can use one of the default datum planes as the mirror reference, and the default datum planes are the most stable references in your model.

Similarly, if you have symmetry, do you model half, a quarter, or one eighth of the part, and then use the Mirror command one or more times?

Regardless whether you have symmetry, another option can be to locate your first solid feature such that the primary, secondary, and or tertiary datum references for Geometric Dimensioning and Tolerancing (GD&T) are aligned coincident with the default datum planes.

Which of these choices are the best? That's another trick question. It depends on your Design Intent: what you want to control and what will provide the most flexibility for anticipated and unanticipated changes later.

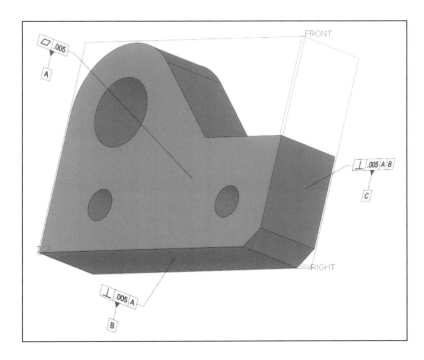

Figure 3-19: First feature located so Datum Feature Symbols align with default datums.

As discussed in section 4.7, a mistake that people make is designing components with reference to a "Universal Coordinate System." In this method, the first feature is located offset from the default datum planes in space. When the component is placed into the assembly using the Default constraint, it is located automatically where it needs to be.

The problem with this method is that it is not parametric. The location of the component fails to update correctly with changes to the assembly. If the product needs to get bigger or smaller, longer or shorter, wider or narrower, then the user must manually open and modify every component defined relative to this "Universal Coordinate System." *This is the opposite of Design Intent.*

To follow proper Design Intent, locate the first feature relative to the part default datum planes and then place it into an assembly using constraints like Coincident, Distance, Parallel, and so on, referencing the appropriate geometry from other components. Alternatively, assemble the component to a Skeleton.

When a change needs to be implemented, change the components or Skeleton as necessary. Any components assembled to them will update their locations appropriately.

3.4.2. Advanced Selection Methods

The basic methods of selecting references in Creo Parametric include:

- Left-clicking on entities in the Graphics Area or Model Tree.
- Using the CTRL key to perform a multi-select.
- Using Query Select (tapping the right mouse button quickly) or Pick From List.

These methods allow you to select explicit references; that is, you are picking a specific surface or edge. However, for certain kinds of features, you can use advanced selection methods, either using the SHIFT key or the Details button in various dashboards. These advanced selection methods are a little more robust than selecting explicit references.

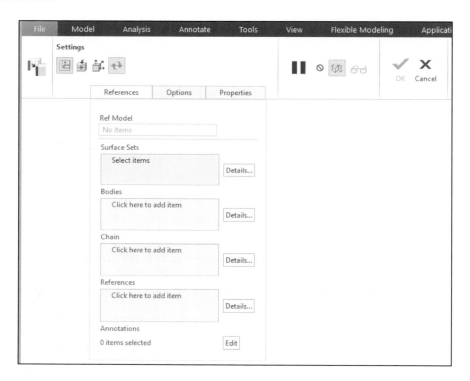

Figure 3-20: Example of Details buttons. The Copy Geometry dashboard.

The types of edge chains are:

- From-To chains.
- Tangent Chains.
- Boundary Chains.

- Surface loops.

The types of surface sets are:

- Solid surfaces.
- Loop surfaces.
- Seed and boundary.

Figure 3-21: Dialog box for constructing Surface Sets with the Details button.

3.4.3. Intent References

There is an even more robust method of selecting references for features like Rounds, Chamfers, and Draft. Rather than selecting specific edges or surfaces, you can select the edges or surfaces associated with a given feature.

For example, let's say you want to apply rounds to the edges of a feature. If that feature is a brick, you could select the top four edges one by one. But supposed the feature changes shape, and instead of a brick, it becomes an extruded racetrack. It is still four edges, but the edges are different. Or maybe it changes to a circle (one edge to pick), or an octagon (eight edges), or some n-sided shape, even including internal loops.

In such a situation, the round would fail to regenerate after the change.

If, however, we picked the Intent References, the round would not fail to regenerate, because we are selecting the edges associated with the feature, not specific explicit edges.

Intent References are selected via Query Select (tapping the right mouse button over the reference until the selection appears) or the Pick from List command.

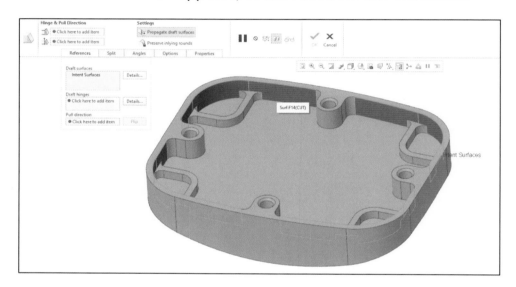

Figure 3-22. Using Query Select to pick the Intent References of a feature to create a Draft feature.

Selecting Intent References is a healthy practice for building robust design models.

3.5.   Feature Order

Creo Parametric is a history-based modeler. Features in parts are regenerated in the order in which they appear in the Model Tree. Changing the order of these features can change our Design Intent.

Consider the following examples:

- A Through All cut removes material from all features that appear after it is in the Model Tree. If a feature is moved above the cut, the cut will not affect it.
- Features with a depth or angle option To Next will have different geometry results depending on which features appear before them in the model.
- Rounds and chamfers propagate to tangent edges by default. If the geometry is added or removed prior to the feature, it can affect the extent of the round or chamfer.

In assemblies, a component can only be assembled to components that appear before it in the Model Tree. If you Edit Definition of a component, all the components that appear after it in the Model Tree will be temporarily suppressed, thus making them unavailable for selection.

Because order and history have such an effect on our models, we need methods to change the order. We do that through Insert Mode and Reorder.

3.5.1. Insert Mode

Sometimes we want to add features or components at an earlier point in our model's history, in other words, higher up in the Model Tree. You'll notice a green bar at the bottom of the Model Tree:

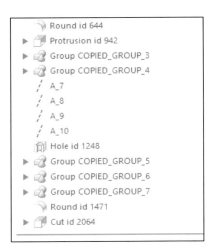

Figure 3-23. Insert Here green bar at the bottom of the Model Tree.

You can drag the green bar up the Model Tree until you reach the point where you want to add more features. The features after the Insert Here arrow will be temporarily suppressed in the model, and a note in the lower left corner of the graphics area indicates that you are in Insert Mode.

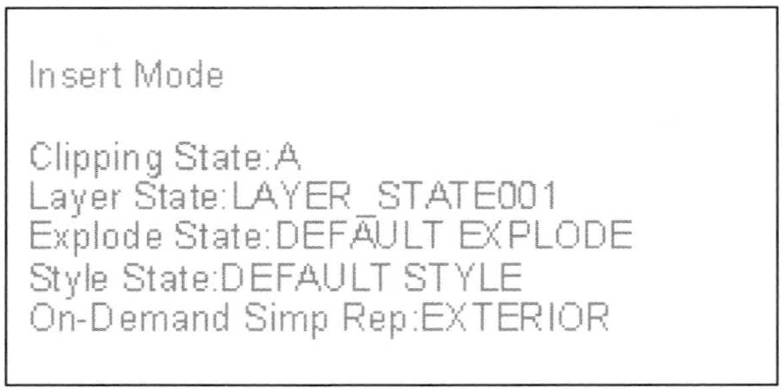

```
Insert Mode

Clipping State:A
Layer State:LAYER_STATE001
Explode State:DEFAULT EXPLODE
Style State:DEFAULT STYLE
On-Demand Simp Rep:EXTERIOR
```

Figure 3-24: Example of text in lower left corner of Graphics Area.

It is a bad practice to save models in Insert Mode. ModelCHECK examines for this condition.

Insert Mode can also be used in assemblies. However, to see the Insert Here arrow, Features must be displayed in the Model Tree. (This is the default starting in Creo Parametric 6.0.)

Dragging the Insert Here arrow can be a pain in the neck in a model that contains a lot of features. As an alternative, you can perform the following steps:

1. Right click the feature after which you want to add features, hold down the right mouse button, and select Insert Here.
2. Create the new features you want.
3. Right click on the Insert Here green bar and select Exit Insert Mode.
4. When prompted to resume features that were suppressed when activating Insert Mode, click Yes.

3.5.2. Reorder

The quick and easy way to reorder features is by dragging and dropping them in the Model Tree. Be aware that you will not be able to reorder a feature before its parents or after its children.

Sometimes it is not always easy to drag and drop the features where you want them to go. In those situations, click Operations > Reorder, which will open the following dialog box:

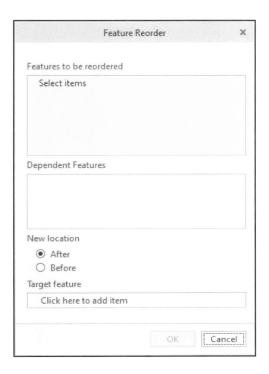

Figure 3-25. Reorder dialog box.

The process is as follows:

1. Select the features you want to reorder using the CTRL key.
2. (Optional) If desired, change the After radio button to Before.
3. Select in the Target feature collector or RMB Target Feature. Then select the feature you want to reorder after or before, depending on which radio button is selected.
4. Click OK.

3.6. Relations

Relations are simply mathematical expressions that relate some dimensions and parameters in your model to other dimensions in your model. Relations add Design Intent to your model because they increase the level of automation.

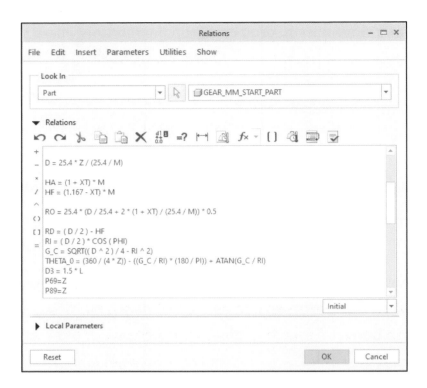

Figure 3-26. The Relations dialog box.

Some situations in which you could use Relations include:

- You want your model to change proportionately. For example, if the length changes, the width should update.
- You have a pattern, and you want the number of instances to update with changes to the model dimensions.
- Your model has mounting locations near the edges of the part, but you do not want to dimension those locations from the edges. You want them dimensioned from a mid-plane or relative to some other reference, but you also want them to update with size changes.
- You have a Family Table, and the features in instances should update with changes to Family Table dimensions.
- You have a template part for generating custom models. For example, a part model uses Pro/PROGRAM or some other input methods to generate bearings, gears, springs, or wave washers.

Although assemblies are not discussed until the next chapter, Relations can also be built between components. For example, you can control the length and width of a lid to change with the size of the opening that it covers.

3.6.1. Types of Relations

There are three main types of Relations that can be written:

- Equality: evaluate an expression and assign the result to a dimension or parameter.
- Comparison: evaluate if something is less than, or equal to, or greater than, or equal to some value or expression. If the result is false, a warning appears in the Message Area during regeneration.
- If – Then – Else: evaluates a condition and determines the actions to follow depending on whether it is true or false.

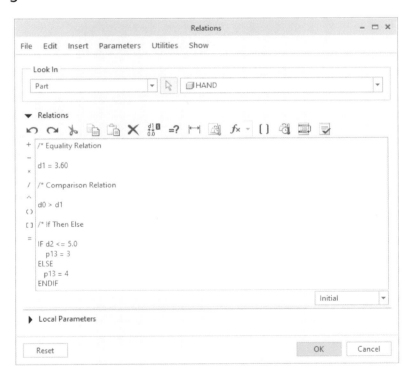

Figure 3-27: Types of Relations.

3.6.2. Advanced Relations Functionality

Relations support a variety of functions, including trigonometric, logarithmic, string editing, mass properties, significant figures, and even cable harness information for use in Relations.

Figure 3-28: Functions available for Relations.

Parameters used in Relations can be assigned units. By default, Relations are unit sensitive, but this can be turned off, as shown in Figure 3-28.

Relations can extract values from a Datum Graph feature for evaluations that cannot be driven by an explicit equation.

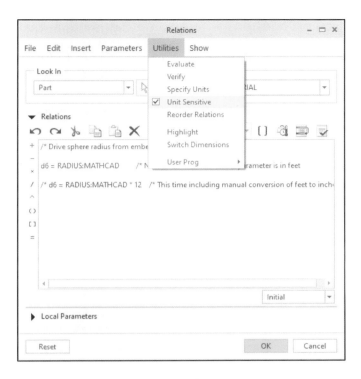

Figure 3-29: Unit Sensitive option for Relations.

3.6.3. Healthy Practices for Relations

Healthy Practices for using Relations include:

- Always precede Relations with a comment line; any line starting with a forward slash and an asterisk (/*). It is frustrating to open up a model with numerous Relations, and then spend significant time figuring out what they do in the model.

- Rename dimensions to make the model user-friendly. See the preceding Healthy Practice.

- Use spaces and blank lines for readability. You may have eagle eyes, but not everyone you work with does.

- Avoid writing Relations in Sketches. This was mentioned in the previous chapter. Relations written at that level can be hard to detect and can leave your model with a permanent yellow regeneration status.

- Do not write Circular Relations where something ends up ultimately being defined by itself. Although Relations are regenerated in order, just like features, Circular Relations can cause errors and result in unpredictable geometry.

Figure 3-30: Circular Relations.

- Be aware of the limitations of Relations written at the assembly level. For better alternatives, see the section on Top Down Design in Chapter 4.
- Most of all, use them! They are a powerful tool for automating how your model reacts to changes.

3.7.   BMX: The Ultimate in Feature Based Parametric Modeling

BMX stands for the Behavioral Modeling Extension. The main functionality in this module includes:

- Datum Analysis Features.
- Feasibility and Optimization Studies.
- Multi Objective Design Studies (MODS).
- Statistical Design Studies.

We will discuss the first two with regard to building Design Intent into parts.

3.7.1. Datum Analysis Features

Datum Analysis Features perform calculations on your model. These calculations can be basic (e.g., length, distance, volume) or advanced (e.g., mass, center of gravity, surface quality). The results of these calculations are parameters and even datum features (e.g., coordinate system at the center of gravity).

Types of Datum Analysis Features include:

- Measure:
  - Distance
  - Area
  - Length
  - Diameter
  - Angle
  - Volume
- Mass Properties for models and cross sections:
  - Mass
  - Surface area
  - Center of gravity
  - Inertia (e.g., inertia tensors, principle moments of inertia, and radii of gyration)
- Geometry:
  - Inside and outside radius of a surface
  - Surface curvature and surface normal
  - Gaussian and section curvature
  - Dihedral angle
  - Deviation
  - Surface slope
- Relations: calculate parameters based on the parameters in your model and/or parameters generated from Datum Analysis Features.
- Excel: pass dimensions and parameters to an Excel spreadsheet, perform calculations on them, and receive the results back.

- Prime / Mathcad Analysis: similar to an Excel Datum Analysis Feature, except this feature passes values to and from a PTC Mathcad worksheet.
- User Defined Analyses: create a custom analysis using a special kind of datum point called a Datum Field Point that is calculated over the domain of a surface or an edge.

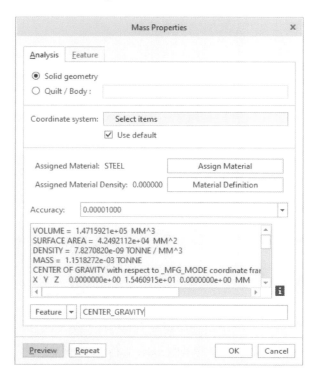

Figure 3-31. Creating a Datum Analysis Feature for a model's mass properties.

3.7.2. Feasibility and Optimization Studies

Feasibility Studies allow you to modify model dimensions within a specified range to drive these calculations to a desired value (e.g., the distance between the center of gravity and my rotation axis should be zero).

An Optimization Study adds a goal minimizing or maximizing some other quantity in your model to the Feasibility Study, to find the best possible result over the solution space. For example, we may want to minimize mass or maximize internal volume.

In other words, we are going to generate the values we want to track, and then get Creo Parametric to make those parameters have the values we want them to have.

Once the values for Datum Analysis Features are calculated, we can set up a Feasibility or Optimization Study, consisting of the following:

- Design Constraints: one of more parameters driven to be equal to, less than, or greater than some specified value.
- Design Variables: model dimensions and parameters that are varied between a minimum and maximum value to meet the Design Constraints.
- Goals (Optimization Studies only): some quantity to be maximized or minimized over the solution space.

Figure 3-32. The dialog box for defining Feasibility and Optimization Studies.

Since these are features in your model they can regenerate whenever the model changes (Since they can take time to process, you might not want them to regenerate all the time).

BMX is the ultimate in feature-based parametric modeling because your part updates automatically to find the optimal solution when other entities in your model change.

3.8.   Other Considerations

This book focuses on the core modeling paradigm behind Creo Parametric: feature-based, history-based parametric modeling. It is not the only modeling paradigm available in CAD. It has its strengths and its weaknesses. To PTC's credit, they address the limitations of feature-based history-based parametric modeling by incorporating:

- Surface modeling techniques that are not hindered by the requirements of parametric modeling; and,
- Direct modeling capability independent of a model's features and history.

In this way, Creo Parametric models become hybrids of the various paradigms.

3.8.1. Industrial Design

Industrial Design (ID) is the art of creating concepts for the shape of products that are visually and artistically appealing. ID is an important, and often early, part of the design process for products like automobiles, consumer electronics, appliances, personal healthcare devices, and so on.

Parametric surface features such as, Boundary Blends and Swept Blends, do not lend themselves easily to these more artistic and aesthetically pleasing pursuits. It is difficult to define the explicit underlying curves for boundaries and trajectories. Also, once created, it is arduous to modify dimensions to get the shapes tweaked into what "feels" right.

Over quite the past few years, Creo Parametric (and its predecessor versions) have moved beyond the traditional, highly defined features into more artistic techniques for Industrial Design. We will discuss two of those techniques: Freeform Surfacing (via the Style feature) and Subdivisional Modeling (via the Freestyle feature).

3.8.1.1. Freeform Surfacing

Parametric surface features require explicitly defined inputs in the form of curves. Constructing curves can be done with a variety of tools including:

- Curve Through Points. This tool requires explicitly defined points, such as points offset from a coordinate system.
- Sketches. These are two-dimensional. Aside from the Spline, Sketches require explicitly defined geometric entities. (A spline requires dimensions on the endpoints only, although the intermediate points can be dimensioned if desired).
- Curves From Equation. These require x, y, and z to be defined in terms of an independent variable t.
- Curves created from an editing tool such as Project, Wrap, Intersect, Offset, and so on, require edges, pre-defined curves, or pre-defined surfaces as inputs.

In other words, defining surfaces using standard parametric modeling can be tedious, difficult, time-consuming, and nearly impossible in some situations. Often, we want to design by "feel," by pushing and pulling points, curves, and surfaces to see the resulting shape immediately.

In Creo Parametric, this is known as Freeform Surfacing via the Style feature in the Interactive Surface Design Extension (ISDX). A Style feature is known as a "super feature" because it contains multiple surfaces and curves.

The Style environment contains a Style Tree similar to the Model Tree. This Style Tree lists the different curves and surfaces contained in the Style feature.

The Style feature has a significant advantage over standard parametric modeling. In Standard Mode, when you edit the definition of an entity, all the subsequent entities in the Model Tree are temporarily suppressed. You cannot see the effect of your change immediately. However, in the Style environment, when you edit the definition of a curve or surface, all the other entities remain visible. The other curves and surfaces update immediately as you make changes to the current entity. This provides real-time feedback regarding the effect of the changes you are making.

The kinds of curves that can be created in the Style environment include:

- Free Curves (3D).
- Planar Curves (2D).
- Curves on Surface.
- Radial Path Planar Curves (curves located on a "soft plane" normal to a curve).
- Drop Curves.
- Proportional Copies.

These curves can be manipulated and controlled. For example, the endpoint conditions can be defined, and internal points can be snapped to geometry.

The kinds of surfaces that can be created include:

- Boundary Surfaces (3 or 4 sides).
- Loft Surfaces.
- Sweep Surfaces.

Surfaces can have G0 (connected), G1 (tangent), G2 (curvature continuous), or G3 (matching acceleration) continuity at their boundaries. The Style environment contains editing tools including Trim and Mirror.

Hybrid modeling combines Freeform surfacing with parametric modeling in the following ways:

- Style curves and surfaces can generate dimensional controls if desired. These dimensions can then be used like other Standard Mode dimensions. They can be edited and used in Patterns or Family Tables.
- Parametric surfaces can use free-form curves as inputs, and similarly, surfaces created in ISDX can use parametric curves as inputs.
- Editing operations from Standard Mode can be applied to Style geometry.

3.8.1.2. Subdivisional Modeling

Creo Parametric supports a technique for designing complex, organic, and aesthetically pleasing surface models that resembles modeling with clay. We start out with a blob of matter, push it, pull it, and refine the shape. It is a very artistic, intuitive method in which we either cannot or do not want to define a full set of dimensions and parameters.

This is known as Subdivisional Modeling. These kinds of models are created within the Freestyle command.

You start off with a lump known as a *Primitive* that has a control mesh surrounding it. You can break up the mesh (subdivide it) and then push and pull the edges and surfaces of the mesh to create the desired shape.

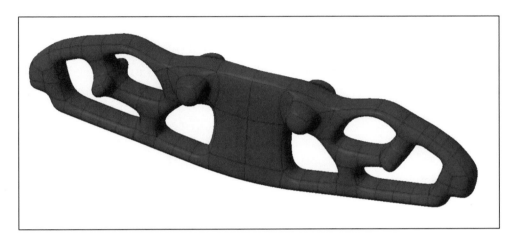

Figure 3-33. Freestyle feature.

Primitives can be 2D:

- Circles.
- Rings.
- Squares.
- Triangles.

Or they can be 3D:

- Spheres.
- Cylinders.
- Cubes.
- Tori (donuts).

Since this is more of an artistic approach, there is no standard uniform process. But the kinds of operations you can perform to achieve your desired geometry include:

- Splitting mesh surfaces and edges.

- Dragging, rotating, and scaling mesh faces and edges.

- Extruding faces.

- Connecting mesh faces.

- Creating hard and soft creases.

- Mirror the mesh about a plane.

Figure 3-34: The Freestyle Ribbon.

Creo 4.0 added the ability to have multiple objects in the same Freestyle feature. To facilitate manipulation, a Freestyle Tree was also added.

3.8.2. The Direct Modeling Paradigm

So far, we have mainly focused on feature-based, history-based parametric modeling, the basis for design in Creo Parametric. This modeling paradigm is characterized by the following:

- Our part models consist of features.
- These features are driven by dimensions and parameters.
- These features have parent-child relationships.
- Our part and assembly models are history dependent; the order in which objects are regenerated affects what geometry is generated.

However, there are alternative paradigms, and these paradigms have benefits at different stages of the design process:

- In the early stages, we may want to iterate numerous concepts for shape and function, without having to define explicit dimensions and parameters that drive the model. We want to generate ideas and geometry quickly.

- In the later stages, we may want to implement design changes without having to understand the models' histories and Design Intent.

The direct modeling paradigm allows you to create and modify geometry without regard to the history of the model and without fully dimensioned and parameterized features.

For Creo Parametric models, there are two ways of using Direct Modeling:

- The Flexible Modeling tab within Creo Parametric.
- The Creo Direct application.

3.8.2.1. Flexible Modeling

The Flexible Modeling tab within Creo Parametric provides two major advantages:

- The ability to modify part models without regard to the history or Design Intent.
- The ability to modify imported geometry that otherwise cannot be changed.

The basic workflow for Flexible Modeling is as follows:

1. Click on the Flexible Modeling tab.

Figure 3-35: The Flexible Modeling tab in part mode.

2. Select an initial surface from the model.
3. Select the additional surfaces you want to modify, using:
   a. The Shape Selection tools.
   b. Geometry Rules.
   c. The right mouse button menu.

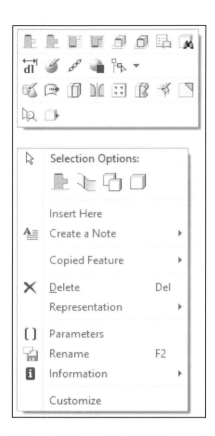

Figure 3-36. Flexible Modeling Mini Toolbar and Right Mouse Button Menu.

4. Apply an action, such as

    a. Move using Dragger.

    b. Move by Dimension.

    c. Move using Constraints.

    d. Edit Round and Edit Chamfer,

    e. Modify Analytic.

    f. Offset.

Flexible Modeling has other powerful tools, including:

- Pattern Recognition allows you to take advantage of Reference Patterns in both part and assembly modes.

- Symmetry Recognition allows changes to an object to be propagated to its mirror.

- Round Recognition and Chamfer Recognition treat geometry as such when changes are made to adjoining geometry.

- Remove behaves similar to the same command in Standard Mode for removing geometry from the model.
- Attach trims or extends quilts to solid geometry.

Operations performed in Flexible Modeling do create features, and like other features, you can use Edit and Edit Definition on them.

3.8.2.2. Creo Direct

Creo Direct is a separate application that creates and uses the same part and assembly models as Creo Parametric.

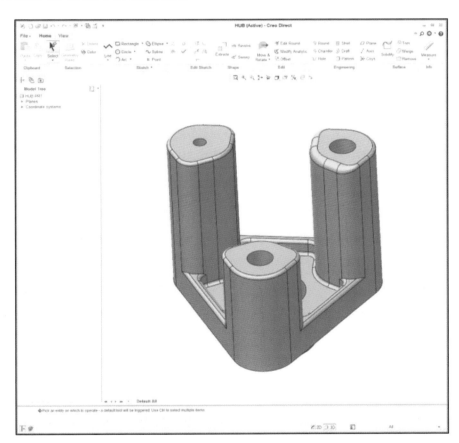

Figure 3-37: The Creo Direct interface.

In part mode, the 2D sketching and 3D tools appear in the same ribbon interface. It contains basic tools only for the quick creation and modification of geometry. The Model Tree contains:

- Datums (Planes, Axes, Coordinate Systems, and Points).
- Quilts.
- Sketches.

Notice that the Model Tree does not contain features. In Direct Modeling, you are not creating features. You are creating and modifying geometry. Accordingly, the Edit and Edit Definition commands do not exist; you modify geometry similar to those commands in Flexible Modeling.

Sketches in Creo Direct have always been able to contain multiple entities, including overlapping entities. When creating an Extrude or a Revolve, you can choose which entities from the Sketch are used. In this way, the same Sketch can be used to create multiple different features. This functionality was not available in Creo Parametric until the 5.0 release.

Assembly constraints do not exist in Creo Direct. In assembly mode, the relevant commands are:

- Insert places a new component in an assembly.
- Position redefines the location of a component in an assembly.
- Move uses a 3D dragger to modify selected geometry in the assembly.

One of the major advantages of direct modeling, though, is that you can perform modifications, like Moves, that affect multiple components.

When those same models are opened in Creo Parametric, the features are exposed in the Model Tree. If a model was modified in Creo Direct, the View Changes dialog box opens. Changes are color coded, and the user has the option of accepting or rejecting them. In assemblies, the parametric behavior is suspended, but it can be restored.

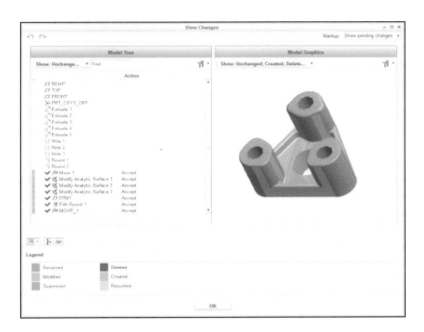

Figure 3-38: The View Changes dialog box.

3.8.2.3. Driven versus Driving Dimensions

Incorporation of Direct Modeling workflows into Creo Parametric has significant impacts on some of the traditional modeling and detailing methods.

The old rule of thumb was that if you were designing your model with Design Intent, then when it came time to create your drawing, there was no need to recreate the dimensions in 2D. Rather than create dimensions, you should simply Show Model Annotations. The old rule of thumb was that at least 95% of the dimensions on your drawing should be driving dimensions that come from your features, with the rest being driven dimensions. You will still find many engineers, designers, and CAD administrators who still espouse this and workplaces that have this as a rule. However, this is up to much debate and may no longer reflect the best ways of working in Creo Parametric today.

(The old advice was that you should not Edit Definition of features merely for the sake of having a driving dimension that you can show on a drawing. This remains true.)

However, here are the developments that make the 95% rule possibly outdated:

- The advent of Flexible Modeling as described in section 3.8.2.1 and 3.8.2.2. Sometimes it is neither possible nor feasible to change features for a drastic change. By using features like Move or Edit Analytic, we might not have dimensions that we can show on a drawing.
- Driven dimensions in Model Based Definition (MBD) contain functionality that driving dimensions do not, such as:
  - The ability to add to Annotation Features.
  - Designation as a Control Characteristic for downstream use in Manufacturing Process Planning (MPP).

I have seen companies and CAD administrators disable the Flexible Modeling tab to prevent users from using driven dimensions in models and MBD. Personally, I think that is a mistake as it robs users of incredibly powerful functionality.

Our tools evolve and gain more capability. We should take advantage of them and rethink our assumptions accordingly.

3.8.3. Design Intent for Additive Manufacturing

Creo Parametric 4.0 introduced the Lattice tool in part mode for creating structures that can be printed using Additive Manufacturing (AM) techniques. At the time of this writing, Creo Parametric is the only CAD package that supports parametric lattices – that is, features that have dimensions and parameters that can be controlled and modified by the user.

3.8.3.1. Lattice Structures

The Lattice feature supports the following types:

- Beam-based. These are 3D cells.
  - The available shapes are:
    - Triangular.
    - Square.
    - Hexagonal.

- Octagonal.
- Stochastic, in which the beam locations determined by randomly distributed points. The available algorithms are Delaunay triangulation (tetrahedra) and Voronai diagram (convex polyhedrons).
  - The user can also control which beams are generated in the cells: horizontal, vertical, angular, truss; inner and/or outer.
- 2.5D, which is an extruded shape. The available shapes are:
  - Triangular.
  - Square.
  - Hexagonal.
  - Octagonal.
- Formula-based. The available functions are:
  - Gyroid

$$\sin(x) \cos(y) + \sin(y) \cos(z) + \sin(z) \cos(x) = 0$$

  - Primitive

$$\cos(x) + \cos(y) + \cos(z) = 0$$

  - Diamond

$$\sin(x) \sin(y) \sin(z) + \sin(x) \cos(y) \cos(z) +$$

$$\cos(x) \sin(y) + \cos(z) + \cos(x) \cos(y) \sin(z) = 0$$

- Custom, in which the cells are defined by a user-defined part.

Dimensions and parameters that can be generated in Lattice features include:

- Cell size, such as the X, Y, and Z dimensions.
- Skewing angle.
- Ball diameter.
- Round radius.
- Cross section size.

These dimensions and patterns can be used anywhere dimensions and parameters are using in Creo Parametric, including but not limited to:

- Family Tables.
- Relations.
- Feasibility and Optimization Studies in the Behavioral Modeling Extension (BMX) as described in section 3.6.

If you design using Additive Manufacturing and Lattice features, be sure to take these advanced capabilities into account when considering how to apply Design Intent.

3.8.3.2. Topology Optimization and Generative Design

Topology Optimization and Generative Design apply Artificial Intelligence (AI) and Machine Learning (ML) to the mechanical design process. Topology Optimization finds the best possible design for a model based on material, boundary conditions, loads, and design goals. It is typically used near the end of the design process to make parts lighter and stronger. Generative Design, on the other hand, is used towards the beginning of the design process to let the software ideate a wide range of potential solutions. Then methods like Pareto are used to narrow the options.

Creo Parametric 5.0 introduced Topology Optimization powered by GENESIS. However, that solver only allowed for geometry that can be created using Additive Manufacturing techniques.

After the acquisition of Frustum by PTC, Creo Parametric 7.0 offers new options for Topology Optimization and Generative Design. (At the time of this writing, the Generative Design functionality has not been introduced.)

Topology Optimization powered by Frustum allows for the creation of geometry with multiple manufacturing constraints, including:

- Additive Manufacturing (AM).
- Traditional CNC machining.
- Injection molding and castings.

When the Generative Design option is introduced in fall 2020, it will use Cloud Computing leveraged from Onshape's Software as a Service (SaaS) functionality.

3.9. How Design Intent Gets Defeated

Some of the ways in which users intentionally or inadvertently defeat Design Intent when designing part models include:

Making choices based on the wrong criteria: In working with users new to Creo Parametric, I have encountered users who have the wrong goals in mind when approaching modeling. The wrong goals include:

- Speed: what is the fastest way to build a part or assembly?
- Simplicity: what methods will result in the fewest number of features or shortest Model Tree?

Lesson: your decisions should always be based on Design Intent.

Getting locked into a standard process: People like standard workflows. It reduces uncertainty and gives us a better sense of confidence. But there is no standard template when it comes to part modeling. You cannot say "always start off with an Extrude as the base feature" and "rounds must never appear in the top quarter of the Model Tree." There are healthy practices to follow for sure, but these are not dogma. If you want to be innovative, you should be aware of the guidelines, but know when to diverge from them.

Relying on too much non-editable geometry: Examples of non-editable geometry include:

- Imported geometry. This can be edited using Direct Modeling techniques. However, tools in the Flexible Modeling tab work better with more prismatic geometry.
- Data Sharing Features like Copy Geometry and Shrinkwrap that cannot be traced back to their source components (due to renaming, data loss, data ownership changes, etc.). This can be difficult or even impossible to modify later.

Multiple entities in a sketch: This is probably the least recommended method in Creo Parametric to duplicate features. Patterns, Mirrors, and Copy & Paste Special provide much more flexible modification opportunities to accommodate future changes.

User-unfriendly models: One of the downsides of Design Intent is that you must have a good understanding of a model's Design Intent to make changes to it. Complex models are difficult to change when users do not do the following:

- Make simple features with a minimum number of Parent-Child Relationships, especially External References.
- Rename features and dimensions.
- Use Local Groups to organize the Model Tree.
- Use spaces and comment lines in Relations.

Saving models with fundamentally bad practices: Models should never be saved (long-term at least, or into data management systems) with any of the following issues:

- Regeneration failures.
- Suppressed objects.
- Insert Mode.
- Circular references.

Overriding dimensions: This is a particular pet peeve of mine and one I believe that should be expressly forbidden at all companies. It is possibly one of the worst practices that can be implemented in a model.

For whatever reason, sometimes people want a dimension reported on the drawing to differ from the values in the model. For similar reasons, they either cannot or will not change the model. This is a technique (which I will not explain because I detest this technique so much) to allow a user to specify a value other than that in the model.

This technique is bad because companies will manufacture the drawing, but are unaware of potential form, fit, or interference issues in the assembly. Similarly, viewables in data management systems like Windchill will be incorrect. While this may be faster or easier for the individual, it is bad for the company and the product.

3.10. Summary

- When selecting what types of features to place in your model, consider what changes are likely to happen. This builds the flexibility in your model to adapt to change and lessen the possibility of having to start over from scratch.

- The choices that you select for the various options in a feature also build Design Intent, especially if they involve selecting other entities in your model.

- Whenever you create a new feature in your model and select existing geometry as references, you are creating a Parent-Child Relationship between the existing entities and the new feature. Changes in our models are propagated via Parent-Child Relationships. Therefore, choose the references for new features carefully.

- Use Intent References when possible. By referencing a feature as opposed to specific surfaces or edges, Intent References are more robust (less likely to fail) than explicit references.

- The order in which our features appear in the model affects what geometry is created. Use Insert Mode and Reorder (drag and drop) to change your Design Intent as necessary.

- If you want dimensions or parameters to change automatically when other dimensions or parameters change, write Relations in your model.

- Datum Analysis Features can perform calculations on your model and generate parameters and other datum features as results. Feasibility and Optimization Studies can then change dimensions in your model automatically to meet your design constraints. This is the ultimate in feature-based parametric modeling, and in building Design Intent at the part level.

- Tools like the Style and Freestyle features provide more artistic, design-by-feel approaches when parametric modeling for surfaces would be too tedious, time-consuming, or restricting.

- The Flexible Modeling tab provides tools for modifying models when you cannot effect the change through the model's Design Intent. This is useful for complex models and imported geometry. Direct modeling complements parametric modeling.

4. Building Design Intent in Assemblies

Key Points:

- We build Design Intent at the assembly level by the choice of the base component, product structure, choice of assembly constraints, and Top Down Design.
- Top Down Design, including the use of Skeletons, Notebooks, and Data Sharing Features, is the most effective method of building Design Intent into assemblies.

4.1.   Overview

If you are reading this book, your end product probably is an assembly (not a part) with a good deal of complexity. More products these days incorporate electronics, software, and internet connectivity. As this level of complexity increases, it is more incumbent on us to build Design Intent into our products.

We build Design Intent in assemblies through the following methods:

- Selection of the Base Component.
- The Product Structure.
- Choice of assembly constraints and connections.
- Top Down Design.

4.2.   Base Component

Assemblies, just like parts, are parametric and have Parent-Child Relationships. When a new component is placed in the assembly, constraints are added to locate it relative to other components. The new component becomes the child of the existing component to which it is assembled, and the existing component is the parent of the newly assembled component.

For this reason, most components in an assembly tend to be related to the first component in the assembly, known as the Base Component. To build Design Intent into the assembly, consider the following when selecting the Base Component:

- Choose a component that is indicative of the size and shape of your model.
- Choose a component to which other components will be mounted.
- Choose something relatively stable (not likely to change much) if possible.

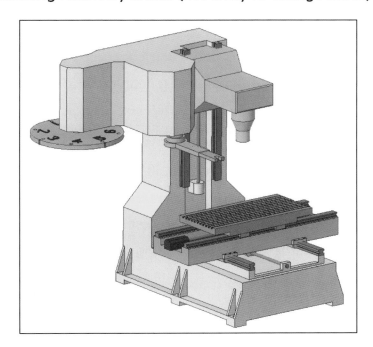

Figure 4-1. The Base Component is sometimes obvious as in this case, but not always.

In an assembly with moving parts (a mechanism), a static component (or what is considered static relative to the rest of the mechanism) is typically chosen as the Base Component.

In a higher-level assembly, the Base Component may be a subassembly.

4.3.   Product Structure

Each subassembly acts as its own distinct, self-contained unit; that is, the assembly constraints that locate the components in the subassembly do not (should not) reference components outside the subassembly. When changes happen to the subassembly, the components therein react together.

Therefore, how we organize our assembly into subassemblies determines how changes are propagated, and therefore determine its Design Intent. This organization of components is known as the *Product Structure*. This is reflected in the Model Tree.

How you define a subassembly depends on many factors, such as:

- Components in the same physical location. For example, in an airplane, we might distinguish between the fuselage, the wings, the rudder, and the elevators.
- Components of the same type. In the same airplane, we might distinguish between structural components and electrical components.
- Components that perform a function (e.g., engine or landing gear).
- Components that are sourced or assembled as a single unit (radar or seat assembly).

The Product Structure is closely related to the Bill of Materials (BOM). The BOM generated from the design assembly is known as the eBOM, or engineering Bill of Materials. The Product Structure and eBOM should be driven from a design perspective, not other concerns like manufacturing, integration, or supply chain.

Later the eBOM can be reorganized and adjusted to create BOMs for other purposes and downstream activities, such as:

- Manufacturing Bill of Materials (mBOM): the reorganization of the eBOM to reflect how the product is actually going to be assembled. The mBOM is an input to Manufacturing Process Planning (MPP).
- Purchasing Bill of Materials (pBOM): reflects sourcing and procurement of components by the Supply Chain. The pBOM is an input to Material Requirements Planning (MRP) / Enterprise Resource Planning (ERP).
- Finance Bill of Materials (generally referred to as "the Fin BOM" and not "the f BOM," for reasons that should be obvious): this is used to generate product cost numbers, factoring in component costs, labor costs, and administrative / overhead costs.

The point is, the Product Structure (eBOM) should be determined by what makes sense design-wise, and how the design assembly should react to change.

4.3.1. Local Groups

Although Local Groups do not affect your Product Structure, they do help to make your model user-friendly and easy to navigate. For example, an assembly could contain a long list of washers, screws, and nuts to fasten components together. This takes up a lot of space in the Model Tree and makes it difficult to read.

To create a Local Group, perform the following steps:

1. Select an inclusive list of components (consecutive with no gaps) using the CTRL or SHIFT keys. (If you select a non-inclusive list, you will be asked if you want to include the features or components in between. If you say no, the operation will abort.)

2. Click the Group icon  from the Mini Toolbar.

3. (Optional but recommended) Rename the Local Group in the Model Tree to make it intuitive and user-friendly.

Membership in the Local Group can be modified by drag-and-drop to add and remove components. The Local Group can also be removed from the Model Tree by selecting it

and clicking Ungroup from the Mini Toolbar.

4.3.2. Restructure

We may wish to change our Product Structure at some point. We may want to move components from one subassembly to another, or to higher or lower-level assemblies. We can make those kinds of changes via a Restructure operation.

Restructure can be accomplished via drag and drop; you can drag components from one subassembly to another, from the top level assembly to a subassembly, and from a subassembly to the top level assembly.

If you have difficulty with drag and drop, perform the following steps:

1. On the Model tab, click on the Component overflow menu and select Restructure.

2. The Restructure dialog box will open. Select the components you wish to restructure; use the CTRL key for multi-select.

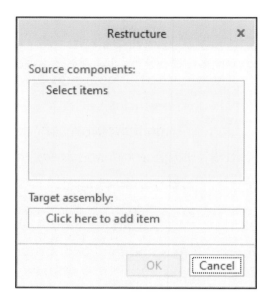

Figure 4-2. The Restructure dialog box.

3. Hold down the right mouse button and select Target Assembly or click in the Target Assembly collector in the dialog box.

4. Select the subassembly or top-level assembly as the destination for the restructured components. Click OK.

Creo Parametric may encounter errors. You may see the following warning:

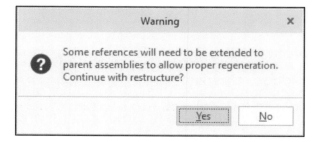

Figure 4-3. Restructure warning.

If the restructure fails, you may want to use the Undo 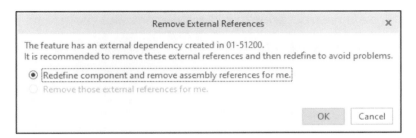 command in the Quick Access toolbar in the upper left corner of the Creo Parametric interface.

Even if the restructure succeeds, assembly constraints remain the same. If you open the subassembly, and Edit Definition of the component, you may see the following warning:

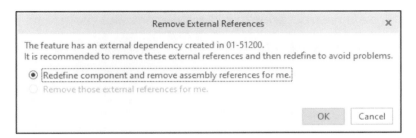

Figure 4-4. Restructure prompt to remove external references.

If you proceed, you will be forced to change the constraints to local references (within the subassembly).

4.3.3. Move to New Subassembly

When working on an assembly, you may decide that a group of components should be its own subassembly. The manual method would be to create a new assembly, place all the components, return to the original assembly, delete the components, and place the new assembly.

To save time and effort, use the Move to New Subassembly command by performing the following actions:

1. Use the CTRL key to select the components you wish to reorganize.
2. Hold down the right mouse button and select the Move to New Subassembly icon.
3. In the Create Component dialog box, enter the File Name and Common Name. Click OK.

4. In the Creation Options dialog box, ensure that the radio button for Copy from existing is selected. If your assembly default template is not listed, use the Browse button to locate it. Click OK.

5. The Component Placement dashboard opens. Hold down the right mouse button and choose Default Constraint. Click the middle mouse button to complete placement.

6. The Model Tree is restructured to reflect the new subassembly. However, the constraints are incorrect. Left click on the base (first) component in the new subassembly and click the Edit Definition icon. Delete the existing constraints or connections. Apply the Default constraint. Click middle mouse button to complete placement.

7. Edit Definition of the new subassembly to apply the previous constraints of the subassembly base component to it.

The process is not currently as automated as we would like. However, it is a valuable tool for updating the Product Structure.

4.4. Constraints

In Chapter 2, we discussed constraints in the context of sketching. Sketcher constraints are rules placed on the geometry, such as, parallel, perpendicular, equal, and tangent.

Assembly constraints are different. In an assembly, constraints define how a component is located.

For static components, we typically define enough constraints to eliminate all the degrees of freedom of the component. For components capable of moving in a mechanism, we typically leave one or more translational and/or rotational degrees of freedom unrestrained.

4.4.1. Default Constraint

Typically, the first component in the assembly (the base component) is located by using the Default constraint. This constraint aligns the default datum planes of the component with the default datum planes of the assembly, locating the component at the origin (the 0, 0, 0 coordinate) of the assembly.

To apply the Default constraint, when assembling a component, simply hold down the right mouse button in the Graphics Area and select Default Constraint. Click the middle mouse button to complete placement.

4.4.2. Fix Constraint

The Fix Constraint locks down a component in space, wherever it is, relative to the default coordinate system.

There are numerous reasons to use the Fix constraint, such as:

- Early in the design stage, the component to which something is supposed to be assembled, doesn't exist yet, or is missing the necessary geometry to add constraints. The Fix constraint can be used to lock the component down temporarily.
- Sometimes you can't define constraints. For example, imported geometry might look cylindrical or analytical, but doesn't get recognized as such when defining constraints.
- Components will get affixed or bonded in an approximate location, so explicitly defined distances from other references aren't necessary. For example, thermocouples, cable tie mounts, zip ties, labels, and other accessory components typically do not require strict placement.

The Fix constraint can be used by itself or in conjunction with other constraints. Be aware, if the references for those other constraints change, it will cause a regeneration failure for the Fix constraint.

To apply the Fix constraint, when placing the component, hold down the right mouse button in the Graphics Area and select Fix Constraint. Then click the middle mouse button to complete placement.

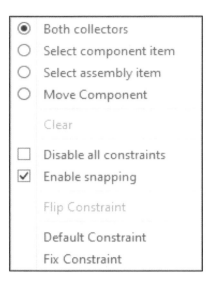

Figure 4-5. Component placement right mouse button menu.

A packaged (underconstrained) component can also be fixed by right clicking on it (in the Model Tree or Graphics Area) and selecting Fix Location.

4.4.3. Assembly Constraints

For static components, it is recommended to add enough constraints to eliminate all degrees of freedom. Components have six degrees of freedom, three translational and three rotational. It usually takes one to three of the remaining constraints to fully constrain a component.

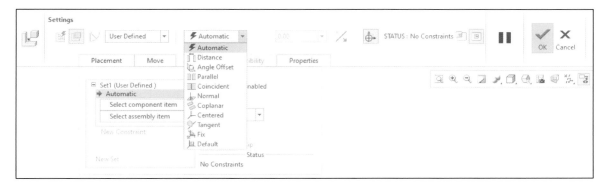

Figure 4-6. Component Placement dashboard for assembling a component with constraints.

Besides Default and Fix, the available assembly constraints are:

- Coincident.
- Distance.
- Parallel.
- Normal.

- Angle Offset.
- Tangent.
- Coplanar.
- Centered.

For some combinations of constraints, the Allow Assumptions option may be available. For components with a rotational degree of freedom, such as screws, washers, and nuts, we do not care about the angle to which a component is rotated. In those situations, we can allow Creo Parametric to assemble at the first possible solution.

Some guidelines for assembling components include:

- When defining constraints, every component referenced creates a Parent-Child Relationship. These should always be minimized. If a component can be fully constrained to only one other component, the assembly will be more stable.
- Assembly constraints should simulate real-world conditions. Assembling to geometry (surfaces) produces better results than assembling to datum planes and axes.
- A component can be over constrained; that is, you can continue adding constraints after it is fully constrained. Sometimes this may be necessary when multiple valid mathematical solutions exist.

4.4.4. Connections

If components are capable of moving, they should not be fully constrained. If the product you are designing is in fact a mechanism (machinery in which motion is used to produce a given result) then the assembly should be designed with *connections* instead of constraints.

There are several healthy – and unhealthy – practices regarding mechanisms. Additional information regarding mechanisms will be covered in the next chapter.

4.5. External References

Before we dive into what External References are, I have to acknowledge how controversial this subject is. There are many companies and individuals who are firmly against their use, often because they have been burned in the past. Granted, when used improperly, they can have severe detrimental effects on your models and your database.

To define External References, first we will discuss Local References. Let's say you are working on a part model. You want to create a hole. You can specify the surface that you want the hole to start from. Then to locate it, you could use a datum axis from the part model. Since these references come from the same part model we are working on, they are Local References.

Say you are working in an assembly. You have two plates stacked on top of each other. Plate A has holes in it, and you want plate B to have holes that match up with the ones in A. When creating holes in B, you could select the axes in A as locating references. Since you are selecting a reference from another model, this is an *External Reference*, not a Local Reference.

(Note that some other software packages refer to this as *Top Down Design* and *Design-in-Context*. These terms have different meanings in Creo Parametric.)

When used improperly, External References can cause serious negative consequences, including:

- Your model fails upon retrieval.
- Geometry cannot be modified later if the original source model cannot be located.
- Retrieving one component causes multiple objects to be pulled into session, thereby slowing down your productivity.
- Your model updates and geometry changes unexpectedly. You especially do not want this happening after the model and/or drawing have been released and is in production.
- If you are using a data management system like Windchill, checking in CAD models with missing references will create "Ghost objects" as placeholders for the missing files.

As mentioned earlier, many companies:

- Forbid the use of External References entirely; or,
- Require all External References to be broken prior to checking into a data management system like Windchill; or,
- Require that External References be broken prior to releasing parts to manufacturing.

External References are powerful, but I recommend they be used under limited and controlled circumstances. In this section, we will discuss the right and wrong ways to employ them. Before you use them, make sure you understand your company's policies regarding them and follow those guidelines.

4.5.1. Direct External References

In our example of creating holes in plate B based on holes in plate A, *we could* simply select the axes in plate A. Some other ways in which External References could be created when designing include:

- When selecting a Sketch Plane or a depth reference for an Extrude, you could select a surface from another model.

- In Sketch Mode, you can select entities from other models as your Sketch References.

- In Sketch Mode, you could use the Project ⬚ Project or Offset ⬚ Offset tools to grab the edges from another part to use in your Sketch.

- Copy and Paste surfaces from one model into another model.

DO NOT USE ANY OF THESE METHODS.

These create what I call *Direct External References*, because you are selecting references explicitly from another model.

In all of these examples, you are creating a required dependency between the parent and the child. Breaking the dependency later can be extremely difficult, or even impossible. You have to ensure that the parent is always retrieved at the same time as the child, or face potential regeneration failures.

If you are going to make External References, they should only be done via Data Sharing features like Copy Geometry, Shrinkwrap, and Merge / Inheritance.

4.5.2. Proper Use of External References

Before you make any External References, ask yourself the following questions:

- Is this absolutely necessary?
- Are there any local references I can use instead?
- Are there no other means of creating this feature?
- Is the intended use of External References proper?
- Am I using this to build Design Intent in my model?
- Am I following practices that allow me to control and break the dependency later?

Guidelines for the use of External References include:

- If you are going to use them, they should be implemented via Data Sharing features. Ideally, they should be done through Skeleton models in conjunction with Top Down Design. These methods are discussed further in Section 4.5.2 on Managing Geometry in Top Down Design.

- Utilize them at the lowest possible level. For example, if you are designing a car and you want to control the location of the posts in the wheel hub assembly and the holes in the wheel, control them in the wheel assembly. Do not control those references at the top level of the car assembly.

- Do not use External References in components that you intend to use in assemblies other than the one you are currently designing.

- Control the dependency of Data Sharing features. By default, they are set to Automatic Update. The Update Control setting can be changed to Manual Update or No Dependency.

- Use the controls available from:
  - Configuration options (File > Options > Configuration Editor).
  - Session options (File > Options > Assembly).
  - The Model Properties dialog box (File > Prepare > Model Properties).

The use and consequences of External References are discussed in more detail in my book *Top Down Design in Creo Parametric*.

4.6. Top Down Design

The traditional method that most people learn first for designing assemblies is Bottom Up Design. First, individual parts are created. Those parts are organized together into simple assemblies. The assemblies are then organized into higher level assemblies. This process continues until the top level of the product structure is created.

Bottom Up Design works perfectly fine in many situations. However, it has disadvantages for complex designs with large numbers of components that are interrelated.

- Managing boundaries between components can be difficult.
- Parts and assemblies often have to be designed in a linear order.

- Modifications require that each individual model be opened and changed one by one.

The general steps in Top Down Design are:

- Create the top level of the assembly first. Then define the major subsystems at the top level, then the subassemblies within those subassemblies, continuing our way down until we arrive at the individual components.
- To control our assembly at the top level and in major subassemblies, we consolidate important design information in special Creo Parametric models.
  - The geometry is defined in special part models called Skeletons.
  - Dimensions and parameters are stored in Notebooks.
- We communicate the design information to parts and assemblies.
  - This geometry in the Skeletons is shared to lower levels via Data Sharing Features.
  - The dimensions and parameters stored in Notebooks are shared via Declarations and Relations.

By having these interconnections between parts and assemblies at the various levels, we gain better control over our assemblies for implementing change. (Warning: Top Down Design does involve more work and setup throughout the design cycle.)

When major and minor changes have to be implemented, rather than opening up dozens or hundreds of individual models to make the change, we can make changes to the top level Skeletons and Notebooks. Regenerating the assembly propagates the changes downward.

If everything works as planned, significant changes can be put into place with considerably less work, and hopefully few to no regeneration failures. (Even with Top Down Design, regeneration failures can happen.)

With Top Down Design, we are controlling:

- Geometry.
- Dimensions and parameters.
- Interdependencies between components.

The tools for implementing Top Down Design include:

- Skeleton Models.
- Engineering Notebooks (known as Layouts prior to Creo Parametric 2.0).
- Data Sharing Features.
- Declarations.
- Relations.

4.6.1. Defining the Product Structure

As stated above, in Top Down Design we build the Product Structure first, starting at

the top level. The top-level assembly is created using the standard New command, from:

- The Quick Access toolbar.
- The File menu.
- The keyboard shortcut CTRL-N.

After initiating the top-level assembly, we define our Product Structure, from the top down as best we know it so far. Essentially, we are defining the Bill of Materials (BOM). We are not focusing on defining features or completing parts.

4.6.1.1. The Component Create Command

Top Down Design makes extensive use of the Create command from the Component group on the Model tab. This opens the Create Component dialog box:

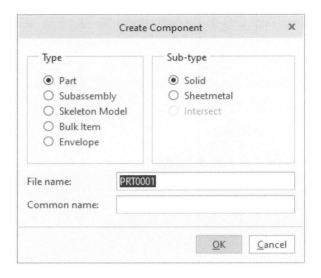

Figure 4-7. Create Component dialog box.

From here, we can create:

- Parts.
- Subassemblies.
- Skeleton Models (discussed in Section 4.5.2).
- Bulk Items. These document consumables that are needed during fabrication and assembly, but do not require 3D models or geometry. These include items such as lubricants, paint, and adhesives.

4.6.1.2. The Assemble Command

Components that already exist can be placed using the Assemble ![Assemble] command with standard constraints or mechanism connections.

4.6.1.3. The Include Command

In the early stages, we may have some items that already have 3D geometry, but we are not ready to define constraints to locate them in the assembly. Perhaps, what they need to be assembled to has not been defined yet. You want it to appear in the Product

Structure / Model Tree, but you do not need the geometry in the Graphics Area. In this situation, you can click on the Assemble drop-down arrow and click Include.

Later when you want the component's geometry to be added to the assembly, use the

Edit Definition command to add standard constraints or mechanism connections.

4.6.2. Skeletons

For complex products, we have a lot of interdependencies between different systems and components. Common areas that need geometry to be shared amongst multiple components include:

- The physical exterior of the product, especially if complex surfacing or Industrial Design (ID) is involved.
- Interfaces between different systems.
- Space claims for components.
- Lines of action and motion envelopes for mechanisms.

To share this geometry, we use a special kind of part model called a *Skeleton*. As mentioned in the previous section, Skeletons are created from the Create Component dialog box in an assembly. They are not created in the same manner as standard part models.

Skeleton Models typically contain:

- Datum Features (planes, axes, coordinate systems, curves, etc.).
- Quilts (surfaces).
- Data Sharing Features (e.g., Copy Geometry, Shrinkwrap) that reference higher-level and parallel-level assemblies.

Solid geometry can be created in Skeleton models. Previously it was recommended that Skeletons contain surface geometry and not solid geometry. However, with the advent of Multibody Modeling in Creo Parametric 7.0, this recommendation no longer holds. Solid geometry in Skeletons will not be included in mass property calculations for assemblies.

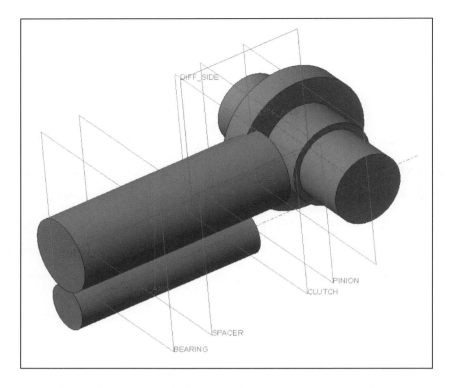

Figure 4-8. Sample skeleton model for a power transmission.

4.6.3. Data Sharing Features

Once we have the geometry in the Skeleton, we use Data Sharing features to communicate this to the subassemblies and component parts that need to reference them. These include:

- Copy Geometry: allows you to select surfaces, curves, edges, and datum features from a single component to use as modeling references.
- Shrinkwrap: allows you to copy all the surfaces from a source assembly.
- Merge: a Boolean addition or subtraction of all the geometry from a source model.
- Inheritance: a one-way associative merge, but with the ability to suppress features and modify dimensions from the original source model.

Update Control enables users to control the dependency for Data Sharing features. The choices are:

- Automatic update. When the source and target models are in session, changes to the source model are propagated to the target model upon regeneration.
- Manual update. This temporarily disables changes from propagating from the source model to the target model.
- No dependency. This permanently breaks the parent-child relationship between the source model and the target model.

Data Sharing features can also contain 3D Annotations from the models they are referencing. These 3D Annotations must be created driven dimensions (Annotation Elements or AEs) within Annotation Features (AF). By sharing these Annotation Elements, users can then show these dimensions on drawings.

Regenerating the assembly updates the Skeleton, which updates the Data Sharing features, which in turn will update any features in parts based on them.

4.6.4. Notebooks

In Section 3.5, we discussed Relations. These are mathematical expressions that control some dimensions and parameters in your model. They can be used at the assembly level. However, if an individual part is open in your Creo Parametric session, but the assembly is not, then the part will not be governed by those Relations at the assembly level. Therefore, Assembly-Level Relations have a critical weakness for managing the values of dimensions and parameters amongst multiple components in an assembly.

In Top Down Design, we can use a special kind of model called a Notebook to solve this problem.

(In Creo 1.0 and earlier, these were known as Layouts. That is why Notebooks have a .lay file extension. These are not to be confused with the .cem Layout files introduced in Creo 2.0. The file extension for Layout files stands for Conceptual Engineering Model).

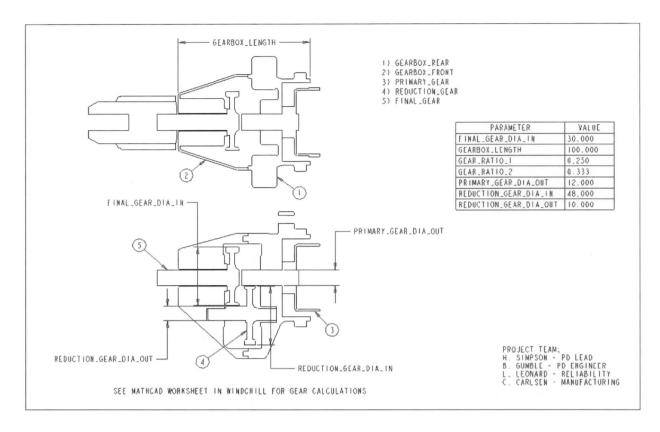

PARAMETER	VALUE
FINAL_GEAR_DIA_IN	30.000
GEARBOX_LENGTH	100.000
GEAR_RATIO_1	0.250
GEAR_RATIO_2	0.333
PRIMARY_GEAR_DIA_OUT	12.000
REDUCTION_GEAR_DIA_IN	48.000
REDUCTION_GEAR_DIA_OUT	10.000

Figure 4-9. Sample Notebook.

A Notebook can contain a variety of different entities, including:

- Dimensions and parameters.
- Non-parametric sketches.
- Balloons.
- Tables, including Repeat Regions to list all Notebook dimensions and parameters.
- Notes.

When a part or assembly is *declared* to the Notebook, all the dimensions and parameters from the Notebook are available to the model. We can now write Relations between the dimensions and parameters from the features in our parts and assemblies using the dimensions and parameters from the Notebook.

The Notebook is automatically retrieved into your Creo Parametric session whenever a model declared to it is retrieved. This way, all the Notebook dimensions and parameters are available. For this reason, Notebooks are superior to Relations at the assembly level.

4.6.5. Resources for More Information

Top Down Design is too large a subject for this e-book. For more information, and an entire book dedicated to Top Down Design, please visit https://www.creowindchill.com or contact me at dmartin@creowindchill.com.

4.7. How Design Intent Gets Defeated

Leaving the Base Component Unconstrained: Sometimes you will retrieve an assembly and find the first component with an empty box next to it in the Model Tree. All the subsequent features have a double box next to them. (These symbols in the Model Tree are known as *glyphs*.)

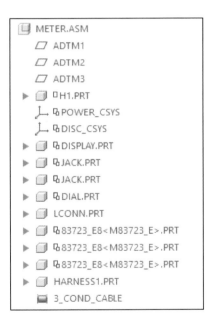

Figure 4-10. Base Component unconstrained.

The single empty box means that the component is underconstrained or *packaged*; it might have no constraints at all. The double empty box indicates that the component is assembled to something that is underconstrained. See Figure 4-16 for more examples of Model Tree glyphs.

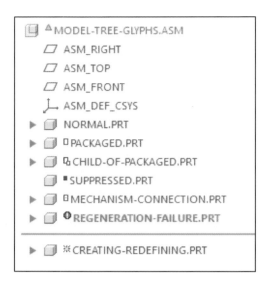

Figure 4-11. Examples of Model Tree glyphs.

In general, the first component will almost always be located using the Default constraint. As mentioned above, the Default constraint removes all degrees of freedom, and locates the component at the origin of the assembly.

Often, editing the definition of the first component to use the Default constraint will end up removing all the Child of Packaged glyphs from all the components.

Assembling a component to more components than necessary: Every component that is used for assembly constraints becomes a parent to the component that is being assembled. By minimizing the number of parents, our models are more robust (less likely to encounter regeneration failures).

Choosing Product Structure based on the wrong criteria: The CAD assembly should be defined by the needs of design and engineering. Although dimensions for Sketches should take manufacturing and inspection into account, the CAD model should not be designed according to how the product will be manufactured or assembled. The Product Structure from the CAD model will generate the Engineering Bill of Materials (eBOM). Later this can be reorganized to generate downstream BOMs for manufacturing, purchasing, planning, and other functions.

Sloppy use of External References. External References are incredibly powerful and an essential part of Top Down Design. But when used incorrectly, they can have severe and disastrous consequences, such as:

- Components can have regeneration failures due to missing references.
- Retrieving components can require an excessive number of other components to be retrieved into session, thereby slowing down your productivity.
- Long regeneration times.
- Components can change when you no longer want them to. This can be a huge problem if the definition changes after the part or assembly has been released.
- When using a data management system like Windchill PDMLink, *ghost objects* can be created when an object with External References is checked in without the source files for those references.

External References should only be used when absolutely necessary. When you must use them, they should be implemented via Skeleton Models and Data Sharing Features.

Defining components in space relative to the default coordinate system: In this technique, components are located exactly where they need to be in the assembly, so they can be placed using the Default constraint. This method, however, cannot accommodate large scale design changes. Components should be assembled to other part geometry or Skeleton Models to update parametrically with changes.

Ineffective use of Libraries to avoid part proliferation: Companies like McMaster Carr provide STEP files and other neutral format files of their components. While this is a good thing, it can result in numerous versions of the same kind of fastener, hardware, or other COTS (Commercial Off the Shelf) parts. Some of these components contain levels of detail that may be unnecessary for your purposes, but result in slow retrieval, regeneration, and repaint times.

4.8. Summary

- Choose the Base Component carefully. Since all components tend to be related in some way or another to the Base Component, changes made to it will be propagated to the rest of the assembly. Therefore, you would want to choose something that hopefully will not change much, and if possible, something that most of the components will be assembled to.

- Organize your product's top level assembly using subassemblies that make sense to the design process. Subassemblies should be self-contained units in terms of how changes should affect them.

- The first component in an assembly should usually be assembled using the Default constraint. Static components should be fully constrained. Components capable of moving in mechanisms should be assembled using connections.

- Top Down Design techniques build Design Intent into large and complex products with interdependencies between the components.

  o In Top Down Design, the Product Structure of subassemblies and components is defined before parts and features are built.

  o Geometry is controlled by consolidating information in Skeleton Models, and then distributing that information into lower level subassemblies and components via Data Sharing Features.

  o Dimensions and parameters are defined in Notebooks. Then models are declared to those Notebooks, so Relations can be written between feature dimensions and the values in those Notebooks.

  o When large changes need to be made, we modify the Skeletons and Notebooks. Upon regeneration, all the dependent models update automatically, saving enormous time and effort.

5. Building Design Intent in Mechanisms

Key Points:

- When components are capable of motion, they should be assembled with the appropriate mechanism connection that allow the appropriate degrees of freedom.
- Basic mechanism connections include Pin, Slider, Cylinder, Planar, Ball, Bearing, and more.
- Advanced mechanism connections include Gears, Cams, Belts, and 3D Connections.
- Tools that support simulation of real-world mechanisms include connections, joint axis limits, and regeneration values.
- Workarounds should be avoided.

5.1. Mechanisms Overview

As mentioned in the previous chapter, when defining the placement for a component in an assembly, you can use either constraints or connections.

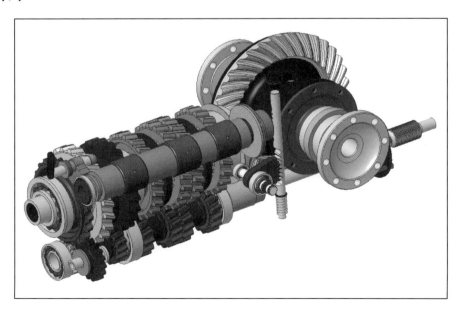

Figure 5-1. Mechanism example incorporating connections, gears, and a rack and pinion.

For static components, you add enough constraints to remove any Degrees of Freedom (DOF). If a component is fully constrained, it is often referred to as *packaged*. However, if a component is capable of motion – it is supposed to translate and/or rotate in one or more Degrees of Freedom – it should be assembled with mechanism connections.

> Note: Every license of Creo Parametric comes with the Mechanism Design Extension (MDX). This enables kinematic studies to determine the position, velocity, and acceleration of components. The Mechanism Dynamics Option (MDO) is required to incorporate dynamic entities like springs and dampers and calculate dynamic results like forces and reactions.

Mechanism connections provide the following advantages:

- You can define references on the component and the assembly for the "zero position" for translation and rotation. Once these are defined, you can then specify minimum and maximum limits as well as the value the model should return to upon regeneration.

Figure 5-2. Additional controls for a mechanism connection.

- Motors can be applied to those connections.
- Kinematic analyses can be run to determine the position, velocity, and acceleration of components.
- Additional outputs and results from analyses include:
  - Graphs of measures.

- o Motion envelopes (parts that represent the volume of space that a component moves through).
- o Movies and animations.
- o Trace curves (2D or 3D datum curves that follow the path of a point or vertex through an analysis).

Figure 5-3. Mechanism mode ribbon.

5.2. Mechanism Connections

5.2.1. Basic Mechanism Connections

Mechanism connections can be defined when assembling the component by clicking on the User Defined drop-down menu on the Component Placement dashboard. The available choices are:

- Rigid.
- Pin.
- Slider.
- Cylinder.

- Planar.
- Ball.
- Weld.
- Bearing.

- General.
- 6DOF.
- Gimbal.
- Slot.

5.2.2. Converting Constraints to Connections

If a component has available degrees of freedom, then its constraints can be converted to the corresponding mechanism connection by clicking the Convert to Connections icon on the Placement dashboard.

5.2.3. Advanced Mechanism Connections

Mechanism mode can be accessed by clicking Applications > Mechanism .
From there, additional advanced connections can be created, including:

- Gears: Generic, Spur, Worm, Bevel, and Rack and Pinion.
- Cam – Follower connections.
- Belts.
- 3D Connections.

Modeling the real-world behavior in terms of how components move inside an assembly will be reflected both in the assembly's regeneration and how it updates when changed.

5.3. Healthy Practices for Mechanisms

Healthy practices when modeling mechanisms include:

- Identify the Ground body. Which component(s) stay fixed during movement or stay fixed relative to the rest of the mechanisms within the subassembly? This is the mechanism's Ground body.
    - Assemble the moving components to the static components.
    - For static assemblies, the Base Component should be indicative of the size and shape of the model. But for mechanisms, the Base Component (Ground) may be something like a clevis or pin that the rest of the mechanism may move around.
    - If a mechanism assembly is a subassembly in a higher-level mechanism, the Ground body in the subassembly may be moving at the higher level. In the subassembly it is the relative Ground about which the other components move.
- Define Zero References and Minimum and Maximum values as appropriate.

- When appropriate, define Regeneration Values in the Component Placement tab. These specify the distances or angles to which components should return initially and at the beginning of every regeneration cycle.
  - Do NOT define these if they do not matter. Setting Regeneration Values can have adverse effects when the mechanism is assembled as a component in a higher-level assembly.
  - Regeneration values can be disabled from the Model Properties dialog box (File > Prepare > Model Properties > Mechanism).
- Limit the number of parents used as placement references, especially for hardware. Users can inadvertently "lock" a mechanism by assembling a moving component to something that is part of Ground, or to an assembly-level datum.
  - As always, if you can limit the component's placement references to only one other component, your assembly will be more stable.
  - This can result in the following error message: "The highlighted connection(s) are not defined from two bodies, if you continue they will be suppressed."
- Lower-level Snapshots and Motors can be used in higher-level Mechanisms to define new Snapshots and initial conditions for analyses.
  - There are known Software Performance Reports (SPRs, also known as bugs) regarding lower-level Snapshots being used in parent assemblies.
  - Therefore, you may want to re-create the Snapshots at the higher level.
- Component Flexibility can be used to manage components like springs and hydraulic hoses. During mechanism analyses and playbacks, the flexible components are suppressed.

5.4. Unhealthy Practices for Mechanisms

Practices for mechanisms that should be avoided include:

- Fully constraining components that should be capable of motion.
- Referencing static Data Sharing geometry in moving components.

- Keeping motion envelopes assembled when the assembly, subsystem, or product is released. Motion envelopes are a design tool and should be removed to maintain BOM integrity.

5.4.1. Component Flexibility

Sometimes people using Component Flexibility as an alternative to mechanism connections. For example, say you have a linear actuator in your assembly. The actuator part has a translational degree of freedom, which would be a Slider connection.

However, sometimes people will assemble the actuator part with a Distance constraint. The linear actuator assembly will be defined with Component Flexibility with the distance value being a Varied Item. The distance will be defined with a numerical value or a measurement.

This is a bad practice. Do not do this. If a component has translational and/or rotational degrees of freedom, it should be defined with connections.

5.4.2. Overloaded BOMs

Another bad technique used for mechanisms is the "Overloaded Assembly" or "Overloaded BOM" (Bill of Materials). This process works as follows:

- Subassemblies with mechanisms are copied into different names.
- The components in the copied subassemblies are positioned to represent different configurations of the mechanism, such as open / closed or retracted / extended.
- Each of these subassemblies is placed into a higher-level assembly. Hence the higher-level assemblies are overloaded with subassemblies.
- Simplified Representations are used to manage the different mechanism configurations and visibility of components.

This technique is particularly bad because:

- The assembly itself is hard to work with because it contains multiple versions of the same subassemblies.
- The subassemblies representing the different configurations are often given names in violation of a company's model numbering standard.
- The mass properties will be incorrect.
- The Bill of Materials will be incorrect.

Simplified Representations are a Large Assembly Management (LAM) tool. They are intended to improve your computer's performance when working on complex models. They should never be used to manage different configurations of an assembly.

There are no advantages to this technique. It should be avoided.

5.5. Design Intent for Mechanisms

When designing mechanisms, think about the motion you are trying to simulate. If you need workarounds or artificial means to replicate the motion in Creo Parametric, you are probably setting up a situation that does not reflect the real world. If you are using some technique to "fake" the mechanism, you are probably defeating Design Intent.

6. Building Design Intent with Multibody Modeling

Key Points:

- Multibody Modeling functionality is available starting in Creo Parametric 7.0.
- Bodies are containers for solid geometry. Every part contains a default Body.
- New Bodies can be created. Features that add solid geometry can be put into new Bodies.
- Boolean operations that can be performed on Bodies include Merge, Intersect, and Subtract. The Split command can divide a single Body into two Bodies.
- Bodies can have their own material assignments and appearances.
- Other operations for Bodies include setting to construction, converting to sheetmetal, and extracting to its own part model.
- Top Down Design and Multibody Modeling complement one another.

6.1. Background and Reason for Existence

6.1.1. History

In the 1980s and most of the 1990s, people used parts they called Master Models and Map Parts for controlling geometry as part of Top Down Design. Since these Master Models and Map Parts were standard part models, you had to filter them out of your Bills of Material (BOM), and any solid geometry screwed up your mass properties.

In the late 1990s, Pro/ENGINEER introduced a new kind of part called Skeletons for Top Down Design. Geometry that defined and affected multiple components was created and controlled in these models. They were filtered from the BOM and any solid geometry did not affect the assembly mass properties. Skeletons, Copy Geometry, and Publish Geometry features formed the core of Top Down Design tools back then.

SolidWorks introduced Multibody functionality as an alternative to Skeletons and Data Sharing features in 2003. CATIA added it in their V5 update. Inventor got similar functionality in 2010.

PTC held out against Multibody for a long time. The reasoning was that you have Skeletons, Data Sharing Features, and Boolean Operations – what do you get from Multibody that you cannot already do? Multibody was, according to some, the weaker workaround.

Finally, PTC decided there was value to this functionality and around 2017 announced they were working on Multibody.

6.1.2. The Case for Multibody Modeling in Creo Parametric

There is one simple reason why Creo Parametric could use Multibody functionality. When you design with solid geometry and one solid intersects another, the exterior surfaces and interior volumes are merged. This was the behavior from Pro/ENGINEER version 1 through Creo Parametric 6.0.

Sometimes when you are modeling a part:

- you do not want intersecting solids to merge.
- you realize that you need to break it up into two or more parts.
- you realize it should be a Skeleton or Master Model.

When you are modeling parts in a relatively small assembly with interdependencies, developing a Skeleton and Data Sharing features can feel like overkill.

6.1.3. Personal Use Cases

In my career, there were three times when the product development organizations I belonged to could have used Multibody Modeling.

Amazon Lab126 is the hardware development arm of Amazon responsible for products like the Amazon Echo, Kindle readers, Fire tablets, and Fire TV. Many of the enclosures are designed for two-shot or multi-shot injection molding due to the advantages for high-volume manufacturing. Without Multibody, you end up designing those enclosures as assemblies. The first shot is its own part. Subsequent parts use Copy Geometry, Shrinkwrap, or direct External References to design the additional shots. Technically, though, the enclosure is not an assembly; this type of manufacturing is intended to avoid assemblies. Designing this way also resulted in adjustments having to be made to the Bill of Materials.

On Amazon Prime Air, sometimes we wanted to design Skeletons with solid geometry for various reasons. But when the solids intersected, they were merged. When we use Copy Geometry features to share the geometry into lower-level Skeletons or individual components, the surfaces had gaps that needed to be filled prior to generating solids.

At Blue Origin, I worked with many tooling engineers. Sometimes in the process of designing fixtures, you realize that a component needs to be broken up into two or more parts. How do you do that with traditional modeling tools in Creo Parametric? How do you split a part into multiple volumes? Do you convert the part model to a Skeleton?

ASIDE: Converting a Standard Part Model into a Skeleton

Many people will tell you that a standard part model cannot be turned into a Skeleton. This is not true. To convert a part model into a Skeleton, perform the following steps.

1. Reorder the part model to be the first object in the Model Tree, even ahead of the Default Datum Planes.
2. Select the part, hold down the right mouse button, and select Replace.
3. Select the By Copy and Copy as Skeleton options.
4. Enter the File Name and click OK.

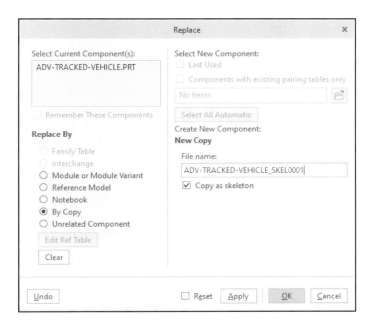

Figure 6-1: Using Replace to convert a part into a Skeleton.

6.2. Use Cases

PTC has identified the following thirteen use cases for Multibody Modeling in the initial release of Creo Parametric 7.0:

1. Multibody part design - Basics
2. Multibody for efficient and flexible part design - Boolean operations with tool bodies
3. Multibody for efficient and flexible part design - Bodies representing subtracted geometry
4. Multibody for efficient and flexible part design - Flexible Modeling
5. Multibody for Additive Manufacturing
6. Multibody for Generative Design
7. Multibody for Simulation
8. Multibody for (Injection Molded) Multi-Material Parts
9. Multibody on Drawings
10. Master Model Methodology with Multibody concepts

11. Multibody for Sheetmetal

12. Multibody support in data exchange

13. Multibody and Windchill, Visualization and ModelCHECK

There is a popular use case that is not yet supported, but PTC is working on. I commonly refer to this as the "PEM use case" or "insert use case." PEM fasteners, also known as self-clinching nuts, and helical inserts are placed into parts, often sheet metal components, so that screws can fasten them to other components. Rather than use an assembly, often people might want to place the PEMs or inserts at the part level, so that the part-level part number reflects the installation of those fasteners during the part's fabrication.

According to PTC, figuring out how this use case integrates with Windchill and Product Structures delays this functionality from being deployed. (By the time you read this, the use case may be supported.)

6.3.   Process

When you create a new part in Creo Parametric 7.0 or open a part created in an earlier version, the Model Tree contains a Bodies folder with a default Body 1. Any solid geometry gets added to the default (active) body.

Additional bodies can be created as desired, and the user can choose which body is the default (the body to which geometry gets added). When a new feature adds solid geometry, the user can create a new body.

The user can perform the following Boolean operations on the bodies:

- Merge.
- Intersect.
- Subtract.

Figure 6-2: Dashboard for Boolean Operations between Bodies.

Additional operations that can be performed on bodies include:

- Split into two bodies.
- Convert to sheetmetal.
- Designate as a construction body so that its geometry doesn't contribute to mass properties or interference checks.

6.4.   Extracting Parts

A new part model can be created from a Body by right clicking on the Body and selecting Create Part from Body from the menu:

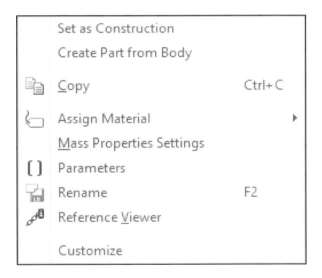

Figure 6-3: Right mouse button menu for a Body.

This will open the New Part from Body dialog box:

116

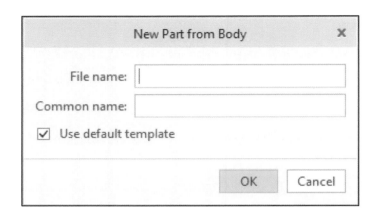

Figure 6-4: New Part from Body dialog box.

Enter the File name and Common Name. Uncheck Use default template if you want to use a different start part. Click OK.

The resulting part will contain an External Copy Geometry feature. If you Edit

Definition  of the External Copy Geometry feature, the Options tab contains the following choices:

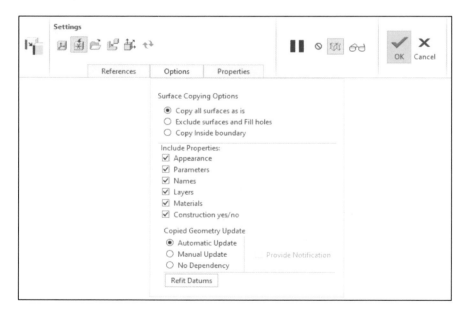

Figure 6-5: Copy Geometry options for Bodies.

By default, the dependency of the External Copy Geometry feature is set to Automatic Update. If the source model and resulting part are in session, the External Copy

Geometry feature will update upon regeneration with changes to the source model. The dependency can be changed to:

- Manual Update. The user must update the External Copy Geometry feature by using either the Update icon on the dashboard or setting the feature to Automatic Update and regenerating.
- No Dependency. This will break the dependency to the source model. This is normally a one-way trip; dependency cannot be re-established later. However, there is a non-recommended configuration option that allows you to re-establish dependency in this situation.

> Note: This is dangerous but setting the hidden configuration option *disallow_restoring_broken_deps* to no allows Data Sharing features set to No Dependency to be changed to Manual Update or Automatic Update. PTC strongly recommends against using this option.

6.5. Multibody Modeling vs. Top Down Design

As I write this, Creo Parametric 7.0 has been available for a few months. I have seen a lot of debates online along the lines of:

- Multibody Modeling is not needed because you have Skeletons and Data Sharing Features in Top Down Design.
- Now that you have Multibody Modeling, you no longer need to use Skeletons, Data Sharing Features, or Top Down Design.

I titled this section so that it is deliberately misleading. This is a false exclusive choice. There is no conflict between Top Down Design and Multibody. The two tools are not mutually exclusive.

You can use Multibody Modeling together or separately. The Master Model Methodology use case specifically provides for the use of Multibody Modeling and Top Down Design together.

Other ways in which the two can be used together include:

- Creating Skeletons with multiple Bodies.
- Multibody parts can have Data Sharing Features including Copy Geometry, Shrinkwrap, and Merge / Inheritance that reference higher-level assemblies or share geometry with components and lower-level assemblies, as well as Publish Geometry features to be shared with other components.
- A standard part model with multiple Bodies can be converted into a Skeleton later.

Situations in which the Multibody process can be easier and more convenient than Top Down Design include:

- Simpler assemblies with interdependencies. Previously I have said designing with Copy Geometry features between parts in assemblies of a dozen components or fewer is perfectly fine. In these simple assemblies, Skeletons can feel like overkill.
- Designing injection-molded multi-material parts as listed in use case 8.
- Accommodating manufacturing processes. For example, you may design an O-ring as a single piece, but then for manufacturing realize that it has to be fabricated in three pieces.

If you were making a Venn diagram, Multibody Modeling and Top Down Design would not be two non-intersecting circles. I do not know if they would be overlapping circles or if the Multibody Modeling circle would be inside the Top Down Design circle. But these are both powerful part- and assembly- design methodologies that should be in your toolbox.

119

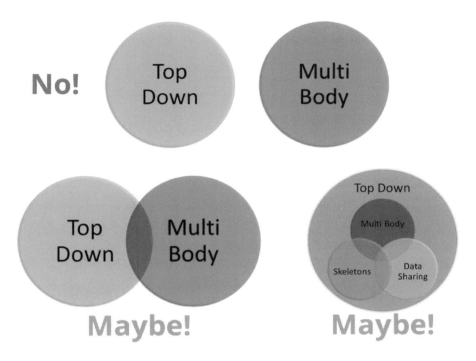

Figure 6-6: Venn diagram for Multibody versus Top Down Design.

7. Building Design Intent with Engineering Calculations

Key Points:

- PTC Mathcad Prime worksheets can be used to build Design Intent via engineering calculations into Creo Parametric models.
- Worksheets created in PTC Mathcad Prime can contain more advanced calculations than are possible with Relations or Notebooks in Creo Parametric.
- The two methods for integrating PTC Mathcad worksheets into Creo Parametric models are with embedded worksheets and Prime Analysis features.

7.1. Engineering Calculations Overview

We already discussed two tools that we can use for capturing our engineering calculations in Creo Parametric:

- Relations.
- Notebooks in Top Down Design, which use Relations.

PTC Mathcad Prime is an application for creating and documenting engineering calculations. We can link our Creo Parametric CAD models to PTC Mathcad Prime worksheets.

Since PTC Mathcad Prime was developed specifically for engineering and math calculations, it contains far more capabilities than the Relations dialog box. These include:

- Over 400 built-in functions in a variety of fields, including differential equations.
- Vector and matrix functionality, including the ability to look up values.
- The ability to read, process, and analyze imported data from sources like Excel.
- Optimization functions for solving and finding minimum and maximum values.

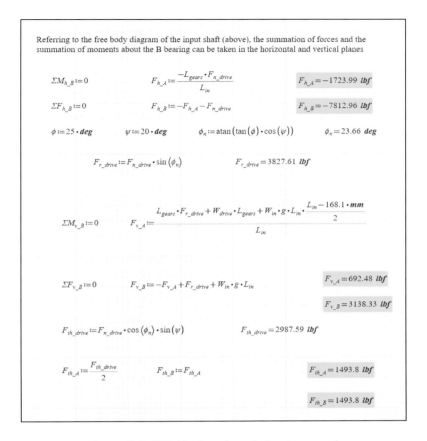

Referring to the free body diagram of the input shaft (above), the summation of forces and the summation of moments about the B bearing can be taken in the horizontal and vertical planes

$$\Sigma M_{h\_B} := 0 \qquad F_{h\_A} := \frac{-L_{gears} \cdot F_{n\_drive}}{L_{in}} \qquad F_{h\_A} = -1723.99 \; lbf$$

$$\Sigma F_{h\_B} := 0 \qquad F_{h\_B} := -F_{h\_A} - F_{n\_drive} \qquad F_{h\_B} = -7812.96 \; lbf$$

$$\phi := 25 \cdot deg \qquad \psi := 20 \cdot deg \qquad \phi_n := atan(tan(\phi) \cdot cos(\psi)) \qquad \phi_n = 23.66 \; deg$$

$$F_{r\_drive} := F_{n\_drive} \cdot sin(\phi_n) \qquad F_{r\_drive} = 3827.61 \; lbf$$

$$\Sigma M_{v\_B} := 0 \qquad F_{v\_A} := \frac{L_{gears} \cdot F_{r\_drive} + W_{drive} \cdot L_{gears} + W_{in} \cdot g \cdot L_{in} \cdot \frac{L_{in} - 168.1 \cdot mm}{2}}{L_{in}}$$

$$\Sigma F_{v\_B} := 0 \qquad F_{v\_B} := -F_{v\_A} + F_{r\_drive} + W_{in} \cdot g \cdot L_{in} \qquad \begin{array}{l} F_{v\_A} = 692.48 \; lbf \\[6pt] F_{v\_B} = 3138.33 \; lbf \end{array}$$

$$F_{th\_drive} := F_{n\_drive} \cdot cos(\phi_n) \cdot sin(\psi) \qquad F_{th\_drive} = 2987.59 \; lbf$$

$$F_{th\_A} := \frac{F_{th\_drive}}{2} \qquad F_{th\_B} := F_{th\_A} \qquad F_{th\_A} = 1493.8 \; lbf$$

$$F_{th\_B} = 1493.8 \; lbf$$

Figure 7-1: PTC Mathcad worksheet example.

However, there is one aspect that really sets PTC Mathcad Prime apart from built-in Creo Parametric functionality for capturing engineering calculations: the ability to document your process and "show your work." Users can place text blocks, text boxes, charts, 2D and 3D plots, and images in their worksheets to explain their decision-making process. All too often this historical information is disconnected from CAD models and the history is lost.

There are two techniques for connecting our models to these worksheets:

- Embedding the worksheet within the model.
- Creating a Prime Analysis feature

Let's take a look at these methods.

7.2. Methods

7.2.1. Embedded Worksheets

As the name states, this method embeds a PTC Mathcad worksheet in a Creo Parametric part or assembly. This is indicated by an icon in the upper right corner of the Graphics Area in Creo Parametric.

Figure 7-2: Creo Parametric indication of an embedded worksheet.

When the worksheet is embedded in the model, PTC Mathcad definition math regions are designated as input variables and evaluation math regions are designated as output regions.

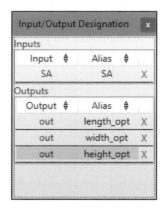

Figure 7-3: Inputs and outputs designated in a PTC Mathcad worksheet.

These inputs and outputs are now available as parameters in the model. Relations are written to:

- assign model dimensions and parameters to the input variables.
- drive model dimensions and parameters from the output variables.

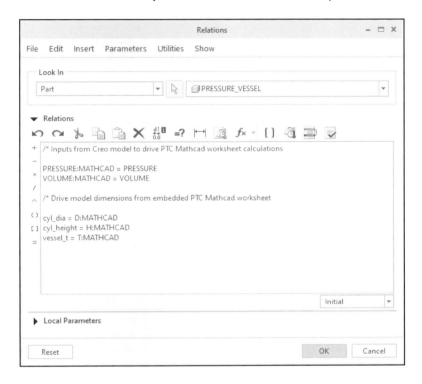

Figure 7-4: Relations for an embedded worksheet.

The Notification Center in Creo Parametric displays a warning when changes to the model result in the embedded worksheet being out of date.

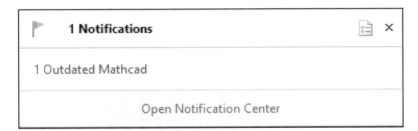

Figure 7-5: Outdated Mathcad worksheet warning in the Notification Center.

The process for updating the Creo Parametric model and PTC Mathcad Prime worksheet is as follows:

1. In Creo Parametric, access the worksheet by clicking Applications > PTC Mathcad > Open / Create Worksheet or double clicking the Mathcad icon in the upper right corner of the Graphics Area.
2. In PTC Mathcad Prime, click Input/Output > Update Inputs.
3. Click File > Save and Push.
4. Return to Creo Parametric and Regenerate the model.

The process of using embedded worksheets is sometimes referred to as "Engineering Notebooks."

7.2.2. Prime Analyses

A Prime Analysis appears as a feature in the model and the Model Tree. It is created from the command Analysis > Prime Analysis, which opens the dialog box seen in Figure 7-6.

The Prime Analysis feature's dialog box contains the following sections:

- A File section that provides access to the external PTC Mathcad Prime worksheet.
- The Inputs section which maps Creo Parametric dimensions and parameters to Mathcad variables.
- The Outputs section which lists the Mathcad output variables and the corresponding Creo Parametric parameters to be created.
- Action buttons to compute the results and create the feature.

The Prime Analysis dialog box also provides control over the units to be used for the inputs and outputs.

Relations are used to drive model dimensions and parameters from the Prime Analysis feature output variables.

Double regeneration (clicking the Regenerate icon twice) may be necessary to update the model's geometry with the results of the Prime Analysis feature. The Regeneration Request option also allows the user to control when the Prime Analysis feature updates.

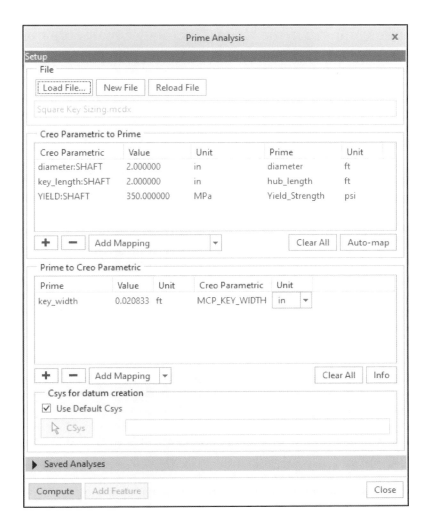

Figure 7-6: Prime Analysis feature dialog box.

7.3. Which Method is Best?

If you have been paying attention, you know that this is both a trick question and not a mutually exclusive choice.

Embedded worksheets have the following advantages:

- You do not need to track an additional file along with the model that uses it.
- The Notification Center informs the user when the embedded worksheet is out of date with the model.
- The user has control over when the worksheet updates the model.

The Prime Analysis feature has the following advantages:

- They appear as features in the Model Tree. They can update every time that the model regenerate; this can be both a pro and a con. It helps to ensure that the model is up to date but can significantly slow down model regeneration.
- They can convert the output variables from PTC Mathcad Prime's system of units to the model's system of units.

The important aspect of using engineering calculations to build Design Intent is that you can capture the complexity, history, and decisions of your product development process. I highly encourage you to explore capturing engineering calculations in your CAD models. You can get started with Mathcad Express, the free version of PTC Mathcad Prime. It can be downloaded from https://www.mathcad.com.

8. Design for Product Variation

Key Points:

- Tools within Creo Parametric can support the manufacturing strategies known as Make to Stock, Assemble to Stock, Assemble to Order, Configure to Order, and Engineer to Order.
- Interchange Assemblies, Component Flexibility, and the Replace functionality support design for product variation within an assembly (below the product level).
- Save As, Family Tables, Configurable Products, and Pro/PROGRAM support design for product variation at the product (top-level assembly) level.

8.1. Product Variation and Data Reuse

Data reuse is one of the primary advantages of using Computer Aided Design tools. Being able to recycle and modify models and drawings can significantly reduce development time, time to mark, product development costs, and product cost.

Henry Ford famously said, "Any customer can have a car painted any color that he wants so long as it's black." That kind of marketplace no longer exists. Customers want – and have come to expect – a high level of choice in their products. This can range from selecting different choices off the shelf to specifying requirements and having a custom product developed from scratch.

There are numerous tools within Creo Parametric to support product variation. Before discussing these tools, we have to understand the various manufacturing strategies used by industry to support product variation.

8.2.   Manufacturing Strategies

Manufacturing Strategies describe the approach to designing, fabricating, integrating, and delivering a company's products to inventory. The choice of strategy depends on numerous factors, including the product's complexity, level of standardization / variation / customization, and lead time. These strategies include:

- Make to Stock (MTS): These are standard components that a company makes without the need for a customer order to be placed. The manufacturing rate is determined through planning based on demand.

- Assemble to Stock (ATS): These products are typically more complicated than those made under the MTS strategy and have such a long lead / final assembly time that they cannot wait until a customer orders them. For example, a car manufacturer will produce a variety of a given line in different colors, transmissions, interiors, navigation packages, and so on.

- Assemble to Order (ATO): a strategy to define product variations from a finite list of option choices. The lead time allows the customer to specify the configuration they want prior to final assembly. For example, once you decide on a computer model, then you can select options for processor, RAM, drives, cameras, and internet connectivity.

- Configure to Order (CTO): product variations are made from a general product with rules and options, as well as limited custom requirements. This represents a higher level of customization than ATO and requires longer lead times. For example, when ordering a custom motorcycle, you can choose engine size, fuel tank size, seats, handlebars, wheels, et cetera. Some of these choices will affect other components, like the frame. In addition, the customer can select custom options like paint scheme and storage compartments.

- Engineer to Order (ETO): This strategy supports the highest level of customization based on the requirements and specifications from the customer. The amount of customization necessitates development work by engineers and designers to ensure that the product will work properly. A customer ordering a yacht can specify the number and types of rooms, length, speed, range, and amenities.

Figure 8-1: Engineered to Order. Photo by Diego F. Parra.

In general, as you proceed down the line of the manufacturing strategies, cost and lead time increase for products within the same class.

Let's look at the tools available in Creo Parametric to support these manufacturing strategies.

8.3.   Methods for Supporting Design for Product Variation

Creo Parametric contains multiple techniques that support varying components within an assembly that needs to define product variations. These techniques include

- Interchange Assemblies.
- Component Flexibility.
- Replace.

8.3.1. Interchange Assemblies

Let's say that you are designing a robot arm for use in manufacturing, and you want it to be able to perform a variety of functions on the shop floor. You want the arm to use a variety of different hands. For example, you may want to swap out 2- and 4- finger grabbers, an arc welding device, a paint sprayer, a screwdriver, a laser measuring device, a camera, and so on.

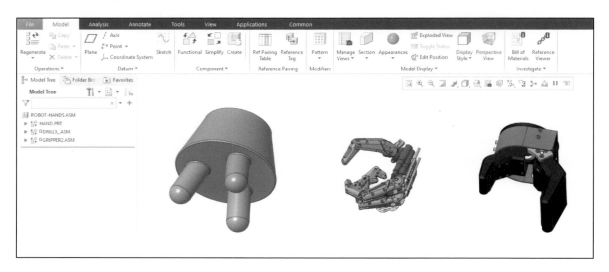

Figure 8-2: Interchange Assembly for robot hands.

These components are too different from one another to be members of a Family Table (as defined in section 8.4.2). Some of the components may be parts and some may be assemblies.

You could use Replace by Unrelated Component (section 8.3.3), but if you are swapping these components frequently, this can be tedious.

Interchange Assemblies solve this problem. An Interchange Assembly is a special kind of assembly model that contains disparate components that can be swapped out for one another. The members of an Interchange Assemblies can be both parts and assemblies. Reference tags define what geometry used to assemble the component and assemble components to them is equivalent in each member.

Interchange Assemblies can be used to support variations in the components in a product manufactured under the ATO, CTO, and ETO strategies.

8.3.2. Component Flexibility

Component Flexibility allows a component in an assembly to vary depending on how that instance of the component appears or is defined in that assembly. One of the most basic examples of component flexibility is a spring. It can have different lengths depending on how it is compressed or extended between its placement references. This allows the component to vary while still retaining the same name and identifying information for downstream Bill of Materials (BOM) and supply chain management.

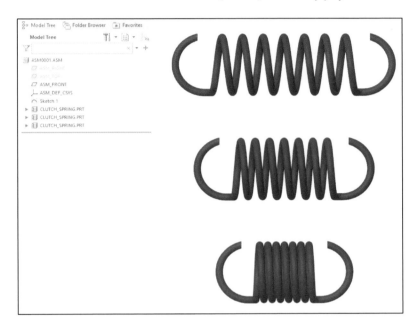

Figure 8-3: Example of Component Flexibility.

For the sake of Product Variation, the more common aspects of a component that can have flexibility applied include:

- Dimensions
- Features
- Components for an assembly
- Materials

Component Flexibility can be defined in the component part or assembly itself or can be applied on the fly when placing the component in an assembly.

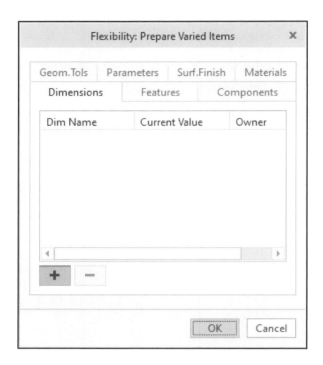

Figure 8-4: Component Flexibility dialog box.

As discussed in section 5.4, Component Flexibility should not be used in lieu of Mechanisms functionality for components with translational and/or rotational degrees of freedom (DOF).

8.3.3. Replace Functionality

Sometimes you have one component in an assembly, and you want a different one in its location. You could delete the component and then assemble the alternative in its place. However, if the component is high up in the assembly's Model Tree, this can have negative ramifications. Deleting the original component could result in multiple regeneration failures.

Instead of deleting the component, the Replace functionality allows one component in an assembly to be swapped out for another component. The Replace function allows you to handle Parent-Child Relationships. You can handle the references in the new component to be used for locating the component in the model. You can also handle the references in the new component necessary for locating the components that are assembled to it.

The methods for replacing one component for another include:

- Family Tables, which are discussed in section 8.4.2.

- Interchange Assemblies, as discussed in section 8.3.1.

- Modules or Module Variants, as discussed in section 8.4.3.

- Reference Model. If models are related via Merge, Inheritance, or Shrinkwrap features, they can be replaced with one another.

- Notebook. Models that are declared to the same Notebook (and preferably are declared to the same Global Datums) can be replaced with one another.

- By Copy. This is like performing a Save As on a component, allowing you to make changes to the copy without affecting the original.

- Unrelated Component. This option facilitates the replacement of one component with, as the name states, a component that has no relationship with the original. The Edit Ref Table dialog box allows you to designate the corresponding placement references between the two components. The components can be saved as an Interchange Assembly on the fly.

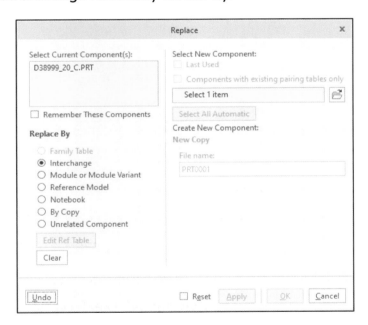

- *Figure 8-5: The Replace dialog box.*

Options will be automatically greyed out as appropriate. For example, if a model is not a member of a Family Table or an Interchange Assembly, those options will not be available.

Given the range of options – especially Replace by Unrelated Component – the Replace command provides almost unlimited capability to swap one component with another for making design changes or product variations.

> Note: the configuration option *remember_replaced_component* controls the creation of a dependency between the original component and the new component. The default value is yes. I recommend setting this to no.

The Replace functionality can be utilized for any of the manufacturing strategies.

8.4.   Methods for Design for Product Variation

Some of the methods for building Design Intent that have already been discussed can be used as part of design for product variation. For example:

- A part can have Relations so that changing certain dimensions and parameters propagate changes to other components, dimensions, and parameters.
- An assembly can be driven by a Notebook that contains Parameter Sets, which drives the values of individual part dimensions for components in an assembly.

However, these are not enough to support building Design Intent into products intended to have variations. In the next sections, we will discuss additional tools in Creo Parametric, as well as their pros and cons, including:

- Save As
- Family Tables
- Configurable Products
- Pro/PROGRAM

8.4.1. Save As

The most basic method of creating a product variation from an existing model is by saving the existing model under a different name. In Creo Parametric, this is performed via the File > Save As > Save a Copy command.

At the part level, the Save As operation allows the user to specify the new File Name for the copy.

At the assembly level, the Save As operations allows the user to specify the new File Name as well as specifying the action to be performed on components within the assembly. These include:

- Reuse.
- Save a Copy.

Figure 8-6: Assembly Save a Copy.

After the Save As operation is performed, the models saved under a new name can be opened and modified as necessary.

Save As is most suited for one-off variations from a source model in which no link is necessary between the original and the variation. Because there is no link, changes cannot be propagated between the models to accommodate changes in Design Intent.

8.4.2. Family Tables

Family Tables are pre-defined variations for a part or an assembly. To create a Family Table, you first design the *generic*, which is the part or assembly model that contains all the various components, features, dimensions, parameters, and other variable entities that can appear in any of the different variations of the generic. These variations are called *instances*.

The different entities that can be varied appear in the Family Table as columns and the entities appear as rows.

The objects that can be varied in a Family Table for a part include:

- Features
- Dimensions
- Parameters
- Merge Part

- Reference Model
- Group
- Pattern Table
- Other

Assemblies contain an additional choice for variation: Components. When a specific component appears as a column in the Family Table, the choices for an instance are:

- Y for yes, indicating that the component appears in the Family Table instance.
- N for no, indicating that the component does not appear in the instance.
- An asterisk, indicating that the instance has the same status as the generic for the component.
- If the component is itself a Family Table generic, the Family Table cell can specify which instance of that component's Family Table appears in the assembly Family Table instance.

Figure 8-7: Assembly Family Table.

The Family Table generic and instances have dependencies between each other. This allows changes to be propagated between them.

For example, changes to the generic have the following ramifications:

- Adding a feature to the generic deletes the feature from all instances as well.
- Deleting a feature from the generic deletes the feature from all instances. If the feature or its dimensions appeared as columns in the Family Table, the columns are deleted as well.
- Changes to dimensions and parameters that do not appear as columns in the Family Table are propagated to the instances.

As discussed in section 8.3.3, instances can be replaced for one another in assemblies.

Family Tables at the product level best support the Make to Stock (MTS) and Assemble to Stock (ATS) manufacturing strategies. At the component level, Family Tables can support all manufacturing strategies.

8.4.3. Configurable Products

A Configurable Product is a special kind of assembly model in Creo Parametric. It can be thought of as an "Overloaded Assembly" or an "Overloaded BOM" (Bill of Materials). It contains all the possible components that can appear in any possible variants of the product.

A Configurable Product can contain:

- Parts.
- Assemblies.
- Configurable Modules.
- Other Configurable Products.

Configurable Modules share a high degree of overlap with Interchange Assemblies. In fact, one can be saved as the other. A Configurable Module contains parts and assemblies that can be swapped out for one another based on the choices in the Configurable Product.

Like an Interchange Assembly, the Configurable Module contains Reference Tags that define the equivalent references between one component or another. These Reference Tags are the geometry used to define how the component is placed into the assembly and how other components are assembled to it.

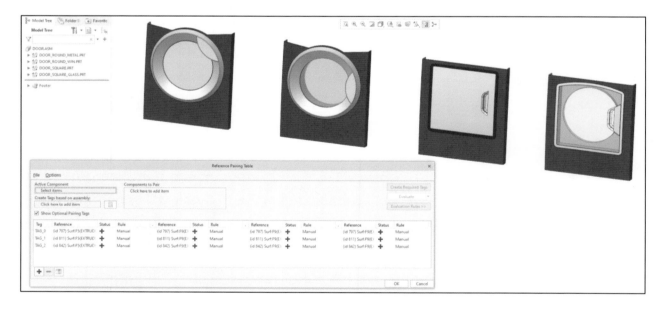

Figure 8-8: Configurable Module with Reference Tags for a washing machine door.

The Configurable Product has different Choices which conform to selections of components from the Configurable Modules.

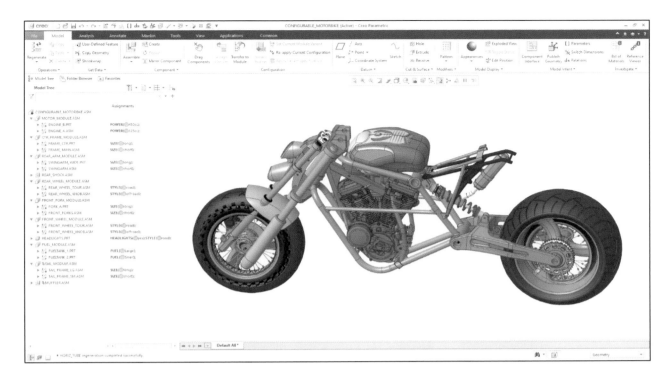

Figure 8-9: Configurable Product with Configurable Module and Choice Assignments.

A Module Variant is the result of the options selected for the various choices and is itself a design assembly.

Configurable Products support the Assemble to Order (ATO) and Configure to Order (CTO) manufacturing strategies.

8.4.4. Pro/PROGRAM

When you regenerate a part or an assembly, Creo Parametric executes the program for that model. The program contains information for the various components and features in the model. The user can access this program and edit it to turn the model's regeneration into an interactive process. During regeneration, the user will be prompted to answer inputs, which are assigned to parameters. The parameters can be real numbers, strings, or yes/no responses.

The program for a model consists of the following sections:

- The Header, with information about the model's type and name as well as Creo Parametric version.

- The Inputs section. Initially this is empty.
- The Relations section. Part- or assembly- level Relations will appear here for parts and assemblies, respectively.
- The Body section. This contains the information regarding the features for a part and components and assembly-level features for an assembly.
- The Mass Properties section.

Customizing the program primarily happens in the middle three sections. The user writes prompts in the Inputs section. The responses to the prompts are assigned to parameters.

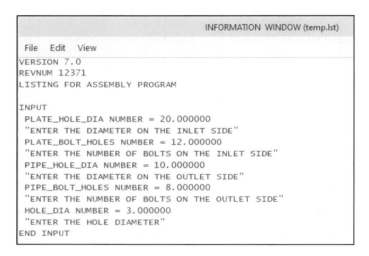

Figure 8-10: Program Header and Inputs sections.

During regeneration, the prompts appear in Message Information Windows at the top center of the Graphics Area.

Figure 8-11: Program prompts during regeneration.

In the Relations section, the user writes Relations to assign the input parameters to model dimensions and parameters.

```
INFORMATION WINDOW (temp.lst)
File   Edit   View

RELATIONS
/* CONTROL THE HOLE DIAMETER IN COMPONENTS BY INPUT VARIABLE

D8:0 = HOLE_DIA
D6:2 = HOLE_DIA
D33:2 = HOLE_DIA
D4:6 = HOLE_DIA

/* LOOK UP CORRECT FAMILY TABLE INSTANCE

BOLT_NAME = LOOKUP_INST( "BOLT.PRT" , 1, "SHAFT_DIA" , HOLE_DIA, "LENGTH", 4 )
NUT_NAME = LOOKUP_INST( "NUT.PRT" , 1, "DIAMETER", HOLE_DIA )
END RELATIONS
```

Figure 8-12: Program Relations section.

The Relations section can also include If-Then-Else structures to compute values.

```
INFORMATION WINDOW (temp.lst)
File   Edit   View

RELATIONS

PIPE_TYPE = "STRAIGHT"
IF ( PIPE_STRAIGHT == NO )
  PIPE_TYPE = "ANGLE"
ENDIF
END RELATIONS
```

Figure 8-13: Program Relations with an If statement.

In the Body section, the user can write If-Then-Else structures around features and components to control the inclusion of those features and components in the model.

If the model is an assembly, values can be passed from the assembly level to components in the EXECUTE commands of the program's body.

```
INFORMATION WINDOW (temp.lst)
File   Edit   View

EXECUTE ASSEMBLY REDUCER-PROGRAM-ASSY
PLATE_HOLE_DIA = PLATE_HOLE_DIA
PLATE_BOLT_HOLES = PLATE_BOLT_HOLES
PIPE_HOLE_DIA = PIPE_HOLE_DIA
PIPE_BOLT_HOLES = PIPE_BOLT_HOLES
BOLT_NAME = BOLT_NAME
NUT_NAME = NUT_NAME
END EXECUTE
```

Figure 8-14: Program sending inputs to a component.

Then in the component's program, those parameters are received as inputs and assigned to the component's dimensions or parameters.

```
                                    INFORMATION  WINDOW (temp.lst)

 File   Edit   View
VERSION 7.0
REVNUM 327
LISTING FOR ASSEMBLY REDUCER-PROGRAM-ASSY

INPUT
 PLATE_HOLE_DIA NUMBER = 20.000000
 PLATE_BOLT_HOLES NUMBER = 12.000000
 PIPE_HOLE_DIA NUMBER = 10.000000
 PIPE_BOLT_HOLES NUMBER = 8.000000
 BOLT_NAME STRING = "BOLT_3_00_L4"
 NUT_NAME STRING = "NUT_3_00"
 HEIGHT NUMBER = 30.000000
 "ENTER THE HEIGHT OF THE REDUCER"
 PIPE_STRAIGHT YES_NO = YES
 "DO YOU WANT A STRAIGHT PIPE?"
END INPUT
```

Figure 8-15: Inputs received from a higher level program.

Other Program functionality includes the ability to select:

- instances from a component's Family Table.
- pre-defined variations of User Defined Features (UDFs).

During regeneration, the user has three choices for responding to the prompts:

- Enter values. If selected, the user chooses which prompts to answer.
- Current values.
- From File.

After regeneration, the user can choose Instantiate to save the result as an instance in the model's Family Table. If the model is an assembly and components were modified by the program, those components will appear as columns in the Family Table and the user will define the name of the instance in the component's Family Table.

Pro/PROGRAM can be used in any design scenarios and support the Configure to Order (CTO) and Engineer to Order (ETO) manufacturing strategies.

8.5. Design Intent and Product Variation

When selecting the methods to use to define product variations, consider the following:

- What manufacturing strategy do you need to support?
- How many different variations do you estimate you need to support?
- What are the ramifications of the methods you select on CAD data management (e.g., Windchill)?
- Which methods provide the most flexibility for adding new variations? Which methods provide the most flexibility for creating the product's next generation or other product lines?
- What changes do you suspect will happen to the base model for generating the variations? Will those changes need to be propagated to the variations?

All products require a manufacturing strategy. Therefore, it helps to take this into consideration as part of your Design Intent.

9. Modifying Design Intent

Key Points

- We often need to modify our Design Intent over the course of a product's development cycle. Tools for changing Design Intent include Edit Definition, Edit Dimensions, Edit References, and Replace References.
- Other methods for changing Design Intent include Reorder, Insert Mode, Parameters, Relations, and Flexible Modeling.

9.1.   Overview

We have covered a variety of tools for defining Design Intent at various levels in our models, healthy practices that promote Design Intent, and bad practices that defeat it. Now we will look at some of the more common commands for modifying the Design Intent in our models.

9.2.   Edit Definition

Since users spend most of their time modifying models than initially creating them, Edit

Definition  is potentially the most used command in Creo Parametric. Edit Definition is a virtual recreate command for your features. When you execute this command, the following occurs:

- The feature displays in preview mode in the Graphics Area.
- Dimensions, drag handles, flip arrows appear for the feature.
- Right mouse button functionality and Mini Toolbars are available.
- The feature dashboard opens at the top of the interface.

Everything about the feature; references, dimensions, dimensioning schemes, options, and attributes can be changed, except for the kind of feature it is.

Because the order of features matters, when editing the definition of a feature in a part, all the subsequent features in the Model Tree are temporarily suppressed. They are no longer visible, thereby preventing users from accidentally selecting a feature that appears after it in the Model Tree as a parent.

In an assembly, when editing the definition of a component to change its constraints, all the subsequent components in the Model Tree are temporarily suppressed.

9.3. Edit

The Edit command allows you to change the values of the dimensions of a feature. In assembly mode, you can also change the value of constraint dimensions for locating components. To edit dimensions, perform the following steps:

1. Either double click a feature or select it and click the Edit icon from the Mini Toolbar.
2. Double click on the dimension and enter the new value.
3. After changing the value of the dimension, double click in the Graphics Area off the model to regenerate the model. Alternatively, click the Regenerate

icon or use the keyboard shortcut CTRL-G.

Another convenient use of the Edit command is to change the properties of a dimension, including:

- Its name. This helps to make the model user-friendly, especially if the dimensions are used in Relations or Family Tables.
- Tolerance mode and values.

146

- Display, such as Basic or Inspection dimension.
- Prefixes, suffixes, additional text, and symbols.

9.4. Edit References

Sometimes a change to a model will result in a subsequent feature losing its parents. Also, sometimes you know that a feature you want to change has children, so prior to making the change, you want to assign those children to alternate parents. The Edit References command is often much faster and easier than Edit Definition.

To use the Edit References command, perform the following steps:

1. Select one or more features or components, either in the Graphics Area or the Model Tree.

2. Click the Edit References icon from the Mini Toolbar. The Edit References dialog box will open:

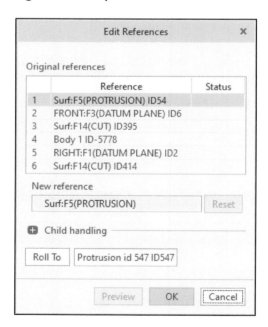

Figure 9-1. The Edit References Dialog Box.

3. (Optional) Click the Roll To button to suppress all objects that appear after the selected objects in the Model Tree. This makes selecting new references easier.

4. If the currently highlighted reference is not the one you wish to reassign, select the appropriate one in the "Original references" list.

5. Select the new reference from the Graphics Area to replace the original reference.

6. (Optional) Expand the "Child handling" list. Check the boxes for other features that use the original reference that you wish to transfer to the new reference.

7. Repeat steps 4 through 6 until you are finished transferring references.

8. (Optional) Click Preview to see the results of your change.

9. Click OK to complete the operation.

9.5. Replace References

Let's say that you need to delete a feature or modify it in some way that surfaces, edges, or other geometric entities are going to be removed from your model. And those surfaces, edges, and so forth, are used as the parents of subsequent features. You are facing quite a few regeneration failures. That's unavoidable, right?

Wrong. Using the Replace References command, you can transfer all the children from the geometric entity that is going away to some other entity that is sticking around.

To use this command, follow these steps:

1. Select the surface or geometric entity in the Graphics Area.

2. On the Model tab, click the Operations overflow menu and Replace References.

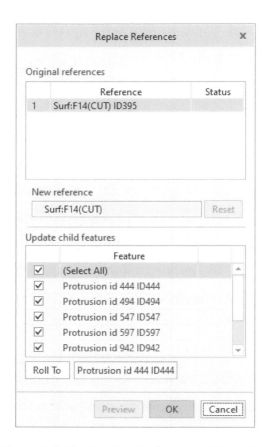

Figure 9-2. The Replace References Dialog Box.

3. (Optional) In the Replace References dialog box, de-select any child features you do not want to transfer.

4. Select the new geometric entity to be the new parent.

5. Click OK.

9.6. Replace in Sketch Mode

Sometimes when deleting entities in Sketch Mode, a Warning dialog box will open:

Figure 9-3. Sketch Mode warning when deleting parents.

Creo Parametric is warning you that you will have a regeneration failure if you proceed. To assign the children of that sketch entity to another sketch entity, there is a Replace command available from both the right mouse button menu and the Operations overflow menu.

To prevent a regeneration failure, perform the following steps to use the Replace command in Sketch Mode:

1. Sketch a new entity that will replace the old entity.
2. Click Operations > Replace.
3. Pick the old entity.
4. Pick the new entity.
5. If you see the following warning, click Yes.

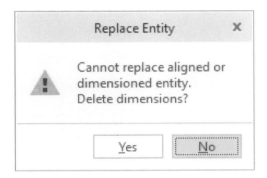

Figure 9-4. Sketch Replace dimensions warning.

9.7. Other Commands

Some of the other ways to change Design Intent in part models include:

- Using Tools > Reference Viewer to examine and break dependencies.
- Dragging the Insert Here green bar to enter Insert Mode.
- Reordering features and components via drag and drop or Operations > Reorder.

- Accessing the Relations dialog box from either Model > Model Intent > Relations or Tools > Relations.
- Accessing the Parameters dialog box from either Model > Model Intent > Parameters or Tools > Parameters.
- Using Direct Modeling techniques by clicking on the Flexible Modeling tab.

9.8.   Summary

- Edit Definition allows you to change everything about a feature including its references, dimensions, attributes, and options.
- Edit allows you to change dimensional values.
- Edit References, Replace References, and the Replace command in Sketch Mode allow you to transfer Parent-Child Relationships from one object to another.
- A variety of other commands are available throughout the various modes of Creo Parametric for implementing changes.

Our Design Intent can change over time. These tools allow us to update our models accordingly.

10. Conclusions

"It isn't what we don't know that gives us trouble, it's what
we know that ain't so."

Will Rogers

10.1. Design Intent Revisited

Building Design Intent into our models is a non-linear process. We never have all the requirements up front. Even if we did, they would change. Design Intent is all about recognizing the inevitability of change, accepting it, and preparing for it. And change is good.

"Without change, there is no innovation, creativity, or
incentive for improvement. Those who initiate change will
have a better opportunity to manage the change that is
inevitable."

William Pollard

Building Design Intent into a model does take more thinking and effort up front. But the more thinking you do in the earlier design stages, the fewer problems you will have later on. The longer a product will be in production and service, the more important it is to build Design Intent into the model.

Every pick and click you make in Creo Parametric is an opportunity to build Design Intent in your sketches, parts, and assemblies or develop a deeper understanding of your models. The payoff in Design Intent is more than reducing frustration or time accommodating changes to requirements.

Design Intent results in models that are more agile; they are able to react quickly to changing requirements.

Design Intent results in *smart, beautiful, powerful models*.

10.2. More Important Than Design Intent

You have just read an entire book about Design Intent, where it's been emphasized that Design Intent should guide every choice that you make in Creo Parametric. Now you get to the end and there is a section titled, "More Important Than Design Intent." What gives?

It's true; since I wrote the first edition of this book, I have come to realize that there are two things more important than Design Intent.

Sometimes people confuse Design Intent with CAD purity. The latter insists on many hard-fast rules that often benefit the CAD system and not the development process. We should have an attitude like Dr. Peter Venkman from Ghostbusters: "I make it a rule never to get involved with possessed people. Actually, it's more of a guideline than a rule."

Adherence to strict and restrictive modeling rules was necessary thirty, twenty, even ten years ago, because computers were less powerful and CAD software was less robust. CAD purity was necessary in many situations simply to get products to open and regenerate, or mesh for analysis, or compute toolpaths.

Design Intent is more important than CAD purity. Two things are more important than Design Intent: the product and the customers.

10.2.1. The Product

In my career, I am tangentially connected to several great products, but there's one that's incredibly successful. I didn't perform any design work on it, but I was the CAD support person at the company when it was released. That product might very well be in your home, and I always get a kick when a television show or some other pop culture references it.

That successful product is great – and it didn't need to have perfect CAD or complete Design Intent. Products are never perfect. Products can be great without having perfect CAD. And some products with perfect CAD, quite frankly, are terrible.

When it comes to product development, the goal shouldn't be perfect modeling, but whether you can answer questions like:

- Is it innovative?
- Does its performance exceed expectations?
- Does it provide a simple, elegant solution to a complex problem?

Good CAD is easier to analyze, manufacture, and reuse, but the emphasis on good CAD shouldn't come at the expense of the product itself.

10.2.2. The Customer

Amazon's Leadership Principles start with Customer Obsession, and that laser focus helps them to rank consistently among the best customer service companies in the world.

The customer is more important than CAD purity and Design Intent. When we focus on the customer, we can create great products. We need to obsess over both *internal customers* and *external customers*.

Your internal customers are your end users and consumers of CAD deliverables. You want to make sure that your end users have the skills and knowledge to use the CAD tool that you provide. I have seen situations where a company's internal processes and rules make their end users hate their CAD tool. No one should find that situation acceptable. The downstream customers of our CAD deliverables need to be able to access and manipulate information – viewables, product structures, metadata – in manners that are efficient for them, and not in terms of what we can give them.

The external customers are, of course, the people who buy and use our products. They don't think about the CAD or any of the other processes that went into delivering the product into their hands. What matters to them is the product and the customer experience.

10.2.3. What Does This Mean to You?

You should not intentionally make bad CAD data or follow unhealthy modeling practices. But your CAD system should be forgiving enough to keep bad modeling from getting in the way of a great product. Your CAD - and Product Lifecycle Management (PLM) - systems should never get in the way of product development.

The CAD is to the product like a screenplay is to a movie. It doesn't matter how good the screenplay is if the underlying story is bad, the movie is poorly made, people don't want to see the movie, and those that do aren't entertained. Never lose sight of what is truly important. CAD and PLM are but means to an end, and that end is happy customers enjoying great products.

10.3. From CAD to CAE

The first edition of this book was written for Creo Parametric 3.0 in 2017. In the time since then, there have been numerous incredible advances to Creo Parametric and Computer Aided Design in general. Especially in Creo Parametric 7.0, we're seeing the combination of seven technologies that were developed separately coming together:

- Multibody Modeling.
- Additive Manufacturing.
- Behavioral Modeling Extension (BMX) for design optimization.
- The application of Artificial Intelligence and Machine Learning to CAD in the forms of Topology Optimization and Generative Design.
- Cloud Computing for Generative Design courtesy of Onshape.
- Real-time simulation via Creo Simulation Live.
- Design Exploration for ideating and branching.

This is an exciting time to be involved in Computer Aided Design. We are experiencing a revolution in which Computer Aided Design has truly become Computer Aided Engineering (CAE). In the past, Creo Parametric (and its predecessor Pro/ENGINEER) primarily followed our explicit instructions for generating 3D models and 2D drawings.

Now Creo Parametric has become an actual design assistant, capable of autonomously generating and optimizing geometry based on the requirements we specify.

With Creo Parametric handling more of the driving and heavy lifting for Computer Aided Engineering, Design Intent is more important than ever.

10.4. Final Comments

I hope this book has helped to demystify why Creo Parametric works the way it does. If you are coming from another CAD software package, maybe you still prefer its workflows, and that's okay. Mastering multiple design packages definitely benefits your career. But having an understanding of the "why" behind the picks and clicks will make you a more proficient user of the software.

Hopefully, this understanding empowers you to create and manage smarter parts and assemblies and helps you on your journey to mastery of design in Creo Parametric. I hope this discussion increases your enthusiasm to design new products that are robust, flexible, parametric, and change the world.

Appendix A: Acronyms

AI	Artificial Intelligence
AM	Additive Manufacturing
ATO	Assemble to Order
ATS	Assemble to Stock
BMX	Behavioral Modeling Extension
BOM	Bill of Materials
CAD	Computer Aided Design
CAE	Computer Aided Engineering
CNC	Computer Numerical Control
CTO	Configure to Order
CSL	Creo Simulation Live
DOF	Degrees of Freedom
DSF	Data Sharing Feature
eBOM	Engineering Bill of Materials
ERP	Enterprise Resource Planning
ETO	Engineer to Order
FMX	Flexible Modeling Extension
ID	Industrial Design
ISDX	Interactive Surface Design Extension
LAM	Large Assembly Management
ML	Machine Learning
MBD	Model Based Definition

mBOM	Manufacturing Bill of Materials
MDX	Mechanism Design Extension
MDO	Mechanism Dynamics Option
MPP	Manufacturing Process Planning
MRP	Material Requirements Planning
OML	Outer Mold Line
ORP	Orientation Reference Plane
pBOM	Purchasing Bill of Materials
PLM	Product Lifecycle Management
SaaS	Software as a Service
SPR	Software Performance Report
TLA	Three Letter Acronym
UDF	User Defined Feature